910094

780.92
GRE   vol 3
                             $25.90

Great Composers

910094
780.92
GRE   vol 3
                             $25.90

Great Composers

Pyotr

Tchaikovsky

1840-1893

Staff Credits

Editors
David Buxton BA (Honours)
Sue Lyon BA (Honours)

Art Editors
Debbie Jecock BA (Honours)
Ray Leaning BA (Honours)
PGCE (Art & Design)

Deputy Editor
Barbara Segall BA

Sub-editors
Geraldine Jones
Judy Oliver BA (Honours)
Nigel Rodgers BA (Honours), MA
Penny Smith
Will Steeds BA (Honours), MA

Designers
Steve Chilcott BA (Honours)
Shirin Patel BA (Honours)
Chris Rathbone

Picture Researchers
Georgina Barker
Julia Calloway BA (Honours)
Vanessa Cawley

Production Controllers
Sue Fuller
Steve Roberts

Secretary
Lynn Smail

Publisher
Terry Waters Grad IOP

Editorial Director
Maggi McCormick

Production Executive
Robert Paulley BSc

Managing Editor
Alan Ross BA (Honours)

Consultants
Dr Antony Hopkins
Commander of the Order
of the British Empire,
Fellow of the
Royal College of Music

Nick Mapstone BA (Honours), MA

Keith Shadwick BA (Honours)

Reference Edition Published 1990

Published by Marshall Cavendish Corporation
147 West Merrick Road
Freeport, Long Island
N.Y. 11520
Typeset by Walkergate Press Ltd, Hull, England
Printed and bound in Singapore by
Times Offset Private Ltd.

© Marshall Cavendish Limited MCMLXXXIV,
MCMLXXXVII, MCMXC

Library of Congress Cataloging-in-Publication Data

The Great composers, their lives and times.

Includes index.
1. Composers–Biography. 2. Music appreciation.
I. Marshall Cavendish Corporation.
ML390.G82   1987   780'.92'2[B]   86-31294
ISBN 0–86307-776-5

ISBN 0-86307-776-5 (set)
     0-86307-779-X (vol)

THE
GREAT COMPOSERS
THEIR LIVES AND TIMES

Pyotr
Tchaikovsky
1840-1893

MARSHALL CAVENDISH
NEW YORK · LONDON · SYDNEY

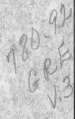

THE
GREAT COMPOSERS
THEIR LIVES AND TIMES

Contents

Introduction

Pytor Il'yich Tchaikovsky's music won immediate popularity among ordinary concert-goers, who responded to its rich emotional textures and lyrical orchestration. Professional critics and musicians were guarded and sometimes hostile in their reactions – Nikolay Rubinstein, the piano virtuoso and friend of Tchaikovsky, initially found the First Piano Concerto 'worthless and unplayable', though he later admitted he had been mistaken. Today both critics and audiences applaud Tchaikovsky's greatness as the composer of some of the most beautiful and well-loved works in the orchestral repertoire.

This volume sets Tchaikovsky's achievement in the context of his life and times. The Composer's Life *begins with a general account of Tchaikovsky's life, then analyzes some aspects of particular relevance: his visit to America at the end of his life, his homosexuality, and finally his curious relationship with Nadezhda von Meck. The* Listener's Guide *discusses some of Tchaikovsky's greatest and best-known works, including the music for the ballets, Swan Lake, The Sleeping Beauty and The Nutcracker, and the 1812 Overture. In the* Background *places Tchaikovsky's life within its historical environment: the changes in Russian society in the 19th century, the contemporary flowering of Russian literature, the history of ballet, and American high society which fêted the composer on his visit in 1891. Tchaikovsky has left us an enduring legacy of great music. By analyzing his life and times, this volume ensures that this inheritance can be fully appreciated and, not least, enjoyed.*

Composer's life

Tchaikovsky's music, with its vivid depiction of desperate unhappiness and extremes of emotion, acts as a mirror to the composer's life. A sensitive child, Tchaikovsky was highly dependent on his mother and never really recovered from the grief he felt when he was sent to boarding school at the age of eight. Her death in 1854 was the final straw, and Tchaikovsky grew into a man who was subject to fits of depression that sometimes threatened to overwhelm him. His emotional anguish was deepened by the shame he felt about his homosexuality and the constant fear of public exposure that haunted him throughout his adult life. His attempt to hide his sexual inclinations by marrying a young admirer, Antonina Milyakova, was a disaster and led to his attempting suicide, followed by a nervous breakdown. In his unhappiness, Tchaikovsky used his music as a refuge, and its melodic expression of emotion inspires the same enthusiastic response from music-lovers as when the works were originally performed.

Pyotr Tchaikovsky

1840–1893

Tchaikovsky was neurotic and deeply sensitive, and his life was often painful and sometimes agonizing. But through the pain shone a genius that created some of the most beautiful of all Romantic melodies.

Pyotr Il'yich Tchaikovsky was born on 7 May 1840 at Votkinsk in Russia, the second son (of five sons and one daughter) of Il'ya Petrovich Tchaikovsky, a mining engineer, and his wife Alexandra Andreyevna. It was clear very early in his life that he had an extraordinary musical talent. At the age of four, with the help of his younger sister Sasha, he composed a song for his mother.

Tchaikovsky's extreme sensitivity was also evident right from infancy. He would over-react to any criticism and so strongly was he affected by music that sometimes the memory of a phrase would keep him awake at night. After one musical evening he was found sitting up in bed crying, 'This music! This music! It's here in my head and won't let me sleep.' A bright child, he learned French and German from a French governess employed by the family, and when he started piano lessons with a local teacher he fast overtook her in his ability at music.

School and Music

When Tchaikovsky was eight, the family moved to St Petersburg where the boy was to spend an unhappy time at the fashionable Schmelling School. It was here that he started his first piano lessons but his musical education was interrupted by a severe attack of measles from which he took six months to recover. As soon as he recovered, in May 1849, the family moved again, to Alapayevsk, but the following year Tchaikovsky's mother sent him back to St Petersburg to enrol in the preparatory class of the School of Jurisprudence as a boarder.

The parting from his mother was one of the most agonizing experiences of his life – he had to be forcibly wrenched away from her, and the horror of that moment stayed with him to the end of his life. The death of a schoolfriend from scarlet fever upset the sensitive boy even more. During an epidemic at his school Tchaikovsky lodged with the boy's family and,

Tchaikovsky was born into a well-to-do middle-class family in their elegant house in Kamsko-Votkinsk (below) – a town in the remote Vyatka province just west of the Urals.

Tchaikovsky's father Il'ya (above), described by the composer's younger brother Modest as being 'jovial and straightforward', was a prosperous manager of an iron mine. He married Alexandra Assier, the composer's mother (above right), in 1833. The influence she had on her son proved to be long and profound.

convinced that he had introduced the disease into the household, believed he was responsible for the death.

In 1852 the family came back to join him in St Petersburg, but his happiness lasted only two years. In June 1854, his mother succumbed to cholera and died. Tchaikovsky, who was very dependent on his mother, was shattered.

His emotional refuge was music. He took singing and piano lessons and through Luigi Piccioli, an Italian singing teacher, learned more about Italian opera. He even toyed with the idea of writing an opera himself, but his first published work was an Italian-style *canzonetta* (short song) called *Mezza notte*.

A musical career

After graduating from the School of Jurisprudence in 1859, Tchaikovsky began working as a clerk for the Ministry of Justice. He hated law, and began seriously to consider a career in music. He attended classes given by Nikolay Zaremba of the Russian Musical Society, soon to become the St Petersburg Conservatoire, and in 1862 started composition lessons with Anton Rubinstein, its first director. The following year, bored with his work at the Ministry, he resigned and joined the Conservatoire as a full-time student.

As well as classes in harmony and composition

When Tchaikovsky was eight his father resigned and the family moved to St Petersburg where winter entertainments included horse and reindeer racing on the frozen river Neva (below and below right).

Tchaikovsky took piano and flute lessons – the latter so that he could play in the Conservatoire orchestra. In 1865 he had the good fortune to have a performance of his *Characteristic Dances* conducted by Johann Strauss, at Pavlovsk, and in the same year he made his first appearance as a conductor in a performance of his Overture in F.

The same year Rubinstein's pianist brother Nikolay, who was about to found the new Moscow Conservatoire, offered Tchaikovsky a job as teacher of harmony. This he accepted, moving to Moscow in January 1866 to lodge with his employer.

Life in Moscow

The gregarious, larger-than-life figure of Nikolay Rubinstein was to dominate Tchaikovsky for many years. Homesick, and aghast at the thought of living in Moscow 'for years . . . perhaps for ever', he found Rubinstein's lifestyle, with its constant 'open house', a little overwhelming, and resented his 'looking after me as if he were my nurse'. No doubt the older man was concerned that his nervous, lonely house-guest and protegé should settle in well, and therefore took pains to introduce him to as many people as possible.

Yet when, in 1868, Tchaikovsky announced that he was in love with the soprano Désirée Artôt, then visiting with an Italian opera company, Rubinstein was among several of his friends who disapproved – probably recognizing that, due to his homosexuality, Tchaikovsky was unlikely to make a satisfactory marriage.

Fortunately, perhaps, for Tchaikovsky, Desirée married another singer, and Tchaikovsky's flirtation was halted – though they remained close friends.

In the meantime, he had composed his First Symphony, which nearly cost him a nervous breakdown. Both of his former teachers, Anton Rubinstein and Zaremba, were among its detractors. But the nationalist group of composers in St Petersburg, nicknamed the 'Mighty Five' (Balakirev, Rimsky-Korsakov, Cui, Borodin and Musorgsky) approved of the first movement when it was heard in 1868. His operas *The Voyevoda* and *Undine*, composed shortly after, met with less success.

Nevertheless, Tchaikovsky was beginning to make his mark on Russian musical society. He had met the music critic Stassov and also Balakirev, leader of the 'Mighty Five', in Moscow in 1868. Balakirev conducted his symphonic fantasia *Fatum* in 1869 and also prompted and advised the composer on the creation of *Romeo and Juliet*.

The beauty of the Russian countryside which Tchaikovsky knew as a boy remained important to him throughout his life. Echoes of the songs and dances of rural Russia can often be heard in his music.

A creative period

By now Rubinstein had moved to a larger house, along with Tchaikovsky, and the stream of visitors continued unabated. Balakirev, Borodin and Rimsky-Korsakov were among the guests, but Tchaikovsky was still consumed with loneliness: what he wanted was an intimate friendship with one special person, and a family atmosphere. He always loved the company of children, and his summers fell into a routine of visits to his married sister Sasha or to his wealthy friend Vladimir Shilovsky at Usovo, and foreign travel. All his life he longed to be elsewhere; yet if he travelled abroad, he was homesick and could not wait to return to Russia. This was, perhaps, another aspect of his search for emotional fulfilment that was never to be satisfied.

By the middle of 1871 he had composed a successful string quartet and was well advanced with *The Oprichnik,* his next operatic work. He also left Rubinstein's household and took a small flat of his own in order to concentrate on composition and he began his Second Symphony.

Professionally, he was doing very well, despite his late start and, had he not been a natural spendthrift, giving away, or financing foreign trips with, whatever income he received, he would have been comfortably off. But he was in torment about his homosexuality. He

At the age of 21, Tchaikovsky joined the St Petersburg Conservatory, where he studied, among other instruments, the flute and organ. During these lean years he supplemented his income by taking on piano and music theory pupils. In 1865, Tchaikovsky (left) graduated and moved the following year to take a teaching post at the Moscow Conservatory.

Reg Wilson

had begun to keep a diary, in which he made frank references to 'this', or 'Z', as well as to his drinking and health.

Returning after a long trip in Europe in 1873 he quickly sketched a new orchestral work, *The Tempest,* and revelled in the beauty of the Russian countryside. All his life, however far he was from his homeland, the thought of rural Russia filled him with patriotic nostalgia. He once wrote, while in Switzerland: 'Surrounded by these majestically beautiful views, and feeling all the impressions of a traveller, I still long for Russia with all my soul, and my heart sinks as I imagine its plains, meadows and woods.'

Back in Moscow, the longing for a true soul-mate returned. There was no one to whom he was really close, though his next orchestral work, *Francesca da Rimini,* his Second and Third String Quartets, his First Piano Concerto and the opera *Vakula the Smith* were to keep him busy over the next few years.

In 1875, Tchaikovsky began writing his Third Symphony and a ballet commissioned by the directorate of the Imperial Theatres in Moscow: *Swan Lake.* The ballet suffered from a poor first performance in 1877; the orchestra found the work difficult in comparison to the trifling pieces they normally played as dance accompaniment, and the audience of the day did not appreciate the brilliance of the score. It was not until after Tchaikovsky's death that *Swan Lake* was to emerge as a great classic.

By his mid-30s, Tchaikovsky had reached a peak of creativity in musical terms, but became more and more troubled by the yawning emotional gap in his life. Seeing marriage as the only way to break with his homosexuality, for which he felt such shame, he wrote to tell his brother Modest, also homosexual, of his decision. He had no idea who his marital partner was to be, but as ill-luck would have it, a candidate was soon to present herself. Yet just before his impending disastrous marriage Tchaikovsky had embarked on an extraordinary relationship with a woman that was to last for 14 years.

Romantic relationships

Tchaikovsky had begun to correspond with an immensely rich widow named Nadezhda von Meck in 1876 while composing his *Variations on a Rococo Theme.* Her husband, an engineer, had made a fortune out of Russia's new railway network, largely due to her business acumen. Now a virtual recluse, Mme von Meck saw almost no one outside her family circle – which, however, often included a 'house' musician (the young Debussy was to be one of them). After Tchaikovsky had executed her first lucrative commission they began to write to each other frequently, soon revealing their feelings and thoughts to each other in a way that neither could have done to anyone else.

Each was determined, because of this intimacy-by-letter, never to meet the other. This arrangement was ideal for Tchaikovsky, for it meant he need never risk the possiblity of entering into a relationship requiring physical passion. It suited her, too, because as long as she never met Tchaikovsky her illusions about him, as her ideal man, could never be destroyed.

Two works occupied Tchaikovsky at this time: his Fourth Symphony, the first of his three great works in this form, which he was to refer to as 'our' symphony in future letters to Mme von Meck, and the opera *Eugene Onegin.*

Distressed by the difficulties he was having with the Symphony, he was surprised one day to receive a

The famous Tatyana Letter Scene (above), from Tchaikovsky's opera Eugene Onegin, *parallels a crucial incident in the composer's own life. In May 1877, he had received an unexpected love-letter from a pupil at the Moscow Conservatory, Antonina Milyukova. More letters followed and eventually, in a state of emotional confusion, Tchaikovsky agreed to meet her. Perhaps mindful of the tragic story of Tatyana, whose love for Onegin is harshly repulsed, Tchaikovsky was moved by Antonina's declarations of love, and married her in July 1877 (right).*

Archiv für Kunst und Geschichte

In 1876, Nadezhda von Meck (above), a resourceful 46-year-old widow, commissioned Tchaikovsky to write an arrangement for violin and piano. She was enraptured with the results and so began a curious patronage and a relationship which virtually excluded their seeing each other. Their prolific correspondence was therapy for them both and totalled 1100 letters.

love-letter from a woman he did not know, Antonina Ivanovna Milyukova, who claimed to be an admirer of his music. More letters followed, with earnest requests that she should be allowed to meet him.

Eventually, perhaps because he was so wrapped up in the tragic story of Tatyana in *Eugene Onegin,* whose love for Onegin is brutally repulsed, Tchaikovsky agreed to meet her, particularly because by this time Antonina had threatened to commit suicide if he refused. Though he told her, when they met, that he could never love her, he later reflected that he had acted thoughtlessly – before he knew what was happening, he had proposed to her and been accepted.

The marriage, which began in July 1877, was a disaster. Antonina's very presence quickly became abhorrent to Tchaikovsky, and to escape her he fled to the Caucasus on the pretext of taking the 'cure'. Mme von Meck, despite her sympathetic letters when he revealed to her his true feelings, was bitter about the marriage, and only too pleased to lend him money to allow him to get away from Antonina.

When he returned, briefly, Antonina boasted of her many former admirers, confident no doubt that her charms would soon have the desired effect upon Tchaikovsky. Yet when Nikolay Rubinstein and Tchaikovsky's brother Anatoly came to inform her that he was a mental and physical wreck, and an immediate divorce was necessary, she received the news with unnatural calm. Her reaction foreshadowed the mental instability which was shortly to assert itself: her sexual obsessions were to result in a succession of illegitimate children by various fathers, and she was to spend the last two decades of her life in a mental asylum.

The divorce, only permissible on the grounds of adultery, was finally granted in 1881, when the first

The city of Florence (below) afforded Tchaikovsky relief from his recurrent bouts of depression. He moved there in 1878 and enjoyed briefly a life of unaccustomed contentment in an apartment rented for him by Mme von Meck. He left the city in 1879 and began a restless nomadic existence, travelling constantly between Russia and the rest of Europe.

child – not the composer's – was born, but Tchaikovsky was to fear public exposure of his homosexuality by Antonina for the rest of his life.

Emotional problems

The mental breakdown he suffered shortly after marrying her was severe. After a bungled suicide attempt, he fled to St Petersburg where he spent two days in a coma. However, the Conservatory granted him a sabbatical and Mme von Meck helpfully bestowed an annuity of 6000 roubles on him to ease any money problems. Anatoly took him off to western Europe for a holiday, where he began to recover his equilibrium. 'Henceforth', he wrote to Mme von Meck, 'every note that emanates from my pen shall be dedicated to you.'

Although he finished *Eugene Onegin,* his finest opera, in San Remo in January 1878, and went on to write his fine Violin Concerto in April, Tchaikovsky was about to enter into a creative doldrums. For years he led an unsettled life, travelling between Russia and western Europe and composing many pieces simply because he had been commissioned to do so rather than from an inner compulsion. The highly popular *1812* Overture was one of these; Tchaikovsky said of it that it was loud and noisy, 'I've written it without affection and enthusiasm', and he feared that there was 'probably no artistic merit in it'.

For almost four years he struggled to begin composing a new symphony. His life fell into a routine. He was now living in a rented house at Maidanovo, near Klin, from which he would sally forth every afternoon after working in the morning. He would take a notebook with him on these 'creative walks', then sort out his ideas during an evening work-session from five to seven. It was Balakirev who inspired his next symphonic work, *Manfred,* based on Byron's verse dream. Tchaikovsky became very depressed while he was working on this but was very pleased with it when he finished it in September 1885.

In 1887 he overcame his fear of conducting enough to conduct, despite agonizing mental strain, the first

When life in Moscow seemed more than Tchaikovsky could bear, the house of the Davidov family at Kamenka (above) provided a much-needed retreat.

Tchaikovsky's sister married Lev Davidov – a renowned revolutionary – in 1861. Of all the beloved Davidov family the composer was most fond of his nephew Bob (front row, near right).

hurt, especially at the implied assertion that their friendship depended on financial support. He wrote immediately to tell her so, but there was no reply. It later transpired that the story of financial ruin was untrue, and it appears that her action was probably triggered by a mental illness from which she suffered for some years. Whatever the reasons, Tchaikovsky's peace of mind was destroyed and he never recovered.

Last years

The following year he began work, without much enthusiasm, on a commission: a ballet based on E. T. A. Hoffman's *The Nutcracker and the Mouse King*. Then, suffering from nervous depression, he set off for Paris, before sailing for New York, to begin a conducting tour. In the French capital he read of the death of his beloved sister Sasha. Arriving depressed and homesick in America, Tchaikovsky's wretched state was relieved a little by the kindness and consideration shown to him by the American people.

In 1893, the last year of his life, Tchaikovsky enjoyed success, popularity and respect to a degree unusual for any composer. He was also at the height of his creative powers, composing the masterly *Pathétique* Symphony during the spring, and completing it, after problems with the orchestration, in August. He was very happy with the work, which he regarded as 'the best of all', and on 28 October he conducted its première in St Petersburg.

A few days later, on 6 November, he was dead. The fear of the public exposure of his homosexuality that had haunted him for so long was finally realized. The threat came, not from Antonina as he had expected, but from a member of the Russian aristocracy with whose nephew Tchaikovsky had had a homosexual liaison. A 'court of honour', including several of Tchaikovsky's contemporaries from the School of Jurisprudence, had decreed that to avert the scandal of exposure Tchaikovsky should commit suicide. Meanwhile, a story was circulated that he died of cholera after drinking unboiled water. He was buried in the Alexander Nevsky monastery in St Petersburg.

The demanding social life of St Petersburg and Moscow (above left) ran counter to Tchaikovsky's yearning for an unmolested life of tranquillity. But he found some peace at Sokolniki, (above right), a cab ride from the city. Here, 'grateful to the Muscovites for not caring for nature' he could take solitary walks.

Tchaikovsky (far right) died under strange circumstances, for long a source of great controversy. Did he die of cholera after drinking unboiled water? Or did he poison himself at the command of a 'court of honour'?

performance of *Cherevichki* ('The Slippers'), and the revised and re-named version of his opera *Vakula the Smith*. In March and November he conducted concerts in St Petersburg and Moscow that consisted entirely of his own works, and they were highly praised. Suddenly, it seemed, he had triumphed over his self-doubts and found the confidence to emerge as a first-rate master of the baton. In 1888 he undertook the first of his conducting tours of western Europe. Hailed everywhere as a great celebrity, he met Brahms and Grieg in Leipzig, Dvořák in Prague and Gounod, Fauré and Massenet in Paris.

Back in Russia he wrote his next masterpiece, the Fifth Symphony and the next year he embarked upon a second international conducting tour and the composition of his second great ballet score, *Sleeping Beauty*, which was first performed in St Petersburg in January 1890.

Tchaikovsky's brother Modest was the librettist of his next opera, *The Queen of Spades,* and like *Eugene Onegin,* the inspiration was a Pushkin tale, with Fate playing a major role in the story. But Fate, too, was once more to intervene in Tchaikovsky's life — again in the form of a letter. This time it was from Mme von Meck, who reported that she was on the verge of financial disaster and could no longer provide his annuity; their friendship must therefore end immediately. Tchaikovsky was amazed and deeply

COMPOSER'S LIFE

A visit to America

The homosexual composer

Tchaikovsky disliked his official life as a Russian composer and escaped by travelling abroad. Once away, however, he was always homesick and, as a sensitive man, found performing and meeting the press and public a great strain. His last foreign trip was in 1891 when he visited the eastern seaboard of the United States, in particular the cities of New York, Baltimore and Philadelphia. At first apprehensive about the response he might expect, Tchaikovsky was overwhelmed by the enthusiasm of American audiences and the lavish hospitality he received. It is certain that Tchaikovsky would not have been such a popular success in America, or any other country, had it been known that he was a homosexual. He always feared public exposure – and with justification since it is probable that his death was suicide following a trial in a 'court of honour'.

'Brave new world'

In the spring of 1891 Tchaikovsky, filled with sadness and apprehension, set off for a month's tour in America. But the New World was full of surprises and his visit was to become a memorable and enriching interlude as his career approached its end.

When Tchaikovsky sailed into New York harbour he was very relieved. The journey had been uncomfortable and tedious and he declared gloomily, 'I simply couldn't bear to stay on board ship any longer'.

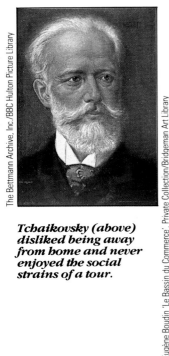

Tchaikovsky (above) disliked being away from home and never enjoyed the social strains of a tour.

Tchaikovsky had sailed for New York from Le Havre (left) on 18 April 1891. He had already been away from home for a month and was suffering frequent pangs of homesickness. His depression was made infinitely worse when, on the day before he sailed, he discovered that his sister had died. Tchaikovsky was deeply fond of Sasha and his brother-in-law (below left) and his first thought had been to abandon his trip and go back to St. Petersburg. He soon realized, however, that it would be useless and would also mean forfeiting a considerable amount of money. So with an exceedingly heavy heart he embarked on his long voyage.

Throughout his life, Tchaikovsky was a compulsive traveller, both inside and outside Russia. Fretting at the constraints of official Russian musical life, he would plan holidays or concert tours to Italy, to France, through Germany and once to England; no sooner had he shaken off his official duties and crossed the frontier than he was lamenting his homesickness and wondering how soon he could be back in his own home again. The furthest he ever ranged was to America, and the experience was important enough for him to devote a special volume of his diaries to it.

In 1891, New York opened its new Music Hall, later to be renamed Carnegie Hall. As conductor of the New York Symphony Society, it fell to the young Walter Damrosch to organize the celebrations; and, taking a chance, he wrote to Tchaikovsky. The invitation fell on unexpectedly fertile ground. Although only just turned 50, Tchaikovsky was beginning to feel his age and was reducing his commitments; but he had recently suffered the setback − both personal and financial − of his patroness Nadezhda von Meck cutting off his allowance. The New World seemed to beckon.

An anxious journey

Characteristically, by the time he was on the boat at Le Havre, he was bitterly regretting his decision. He had just received news of the death of his beloved sister Alexandra, and his gloom was not alleviated when a young man committed suicide by leaping off the ship. He was also stuck with his new ballet, *The Nutcracker,* 'being completely at a loss as to how to portray the Sugar Plum Fairy in music'. Perhaps partly to feel a continuing sense of contact with home, and also to lighten the burden of letter-writing, he turned to his diary and first, to a long diary-letter to his brother Modest.

It reveals much about the trip. Always obsessively fussy about the detail of his life, Tchaikovsky was also a perceptive observer and an honest reporter. He took an instant dislike to the American family with whom he found himself dining; however, he liked the ship, the *Bretagne,* which he described as no less than 'a floating palace'. His new assurance about the journey, as they sailed calmly past the Lizard, was dispelled the next morning when they hit the Atlantic swell. However, the weather reduced the numbers of people to be seen on deck − there were some 80 first-class passengers − and he discovered to his relief that he was not prone to seasickness. There was even pleasure to be found in the sight of the surging waves and the gulls blowing across the ship. Spirits were reduced again when a young man from the second class with whom he had struck up a friendship, and to whom he had confided his tendency to depression, remarked consolingly 'Well, at your age it's only natural.'

As the weather grew calmer, more passengers were visible, and it was not long before their distinguished companion was recognized. Earlier, he had endured in silence a 'Miss' singing Italian songs at the piano so badly that he failed to understand why she had met with such a friendly reception; now, he was himself pressed to oblige, and found it in the end simpler to give in. Other worries included the possibility of collision as fog descended, though the irritation of the siren being continually sounded was hardly less troublesome. Brandy and coffee saw him through the worst of his anxieties; but it was a considerable relief when he was able to end his long letter to Modest with the news that they had docked safely. 'New York is a very beautiful and very unusual city. On the main streets there are single-storeyed little houses side by side with buildings nine storeys high.'

Overwhelming hospitality

American hospitality immediately engulfed the anxious composer. He was much impressed with his own ability to carry on an animated conversation with the friendly reception committee which met him and drove him to the Hotel Normandie – 'but in my soul there was despair and a desire to flee from them to the world's end'. However, not only his good manners but his genuine appreciation of their kindness triumphed, and a keynote of the diaries is his interest in the novel sights of America – he seems not to have expected so many black people, or such a high standard of creature comforts. This offset the private gloom that often had him weeping alone in his room.

Those chiefly responsible for looking after Tchaikovsky in New York were Morris Reno, president of the Music Hall Company, and Ferdinand Mayer, of the Knabe Piano Company, as well as Walter Damrosch. They seem to have been both attentive and discreet, anxious to see that he was well looked after while also protecting him from difficulties. A persistent reporter, 'some of whose questions were very curious', was kept from his worst importunities by Mayer, who interpreted by way of German. Mayer then took Tchaikovsky off to the rehearsal.

At the rehearsal they were finishing the finale of Beethoven's Fifth Symphony. Damrosch (conducting without a frock coat) seemed to me very charming. At the finish of the symphony I started to go to him but I had to stop immediately to respond to the loud greetings of the orchestra. Damrosch delivered another speech; another ovation. I succeeded in rehearsing only the first and third movements of the Third Suite. The orchestra is splendid.

Walter Damrosch (above) invited Tchaikovsky to New York to appear in the opening concerts at the New York Music Hall. Tchaikovsky's phenomenal success prompted him to comment that it seemed he was better known in America than in Russia.

Tchaikovsky strolled down Broadway (right) on his first night in New York and wrote in incredulous tones to his brother about the height of the buildings. He also remarked **upon the number of 'negro faces' to be seen in the streets. The Cake Walk (above) was a black dance of the time which was becoming popular throughout America.**

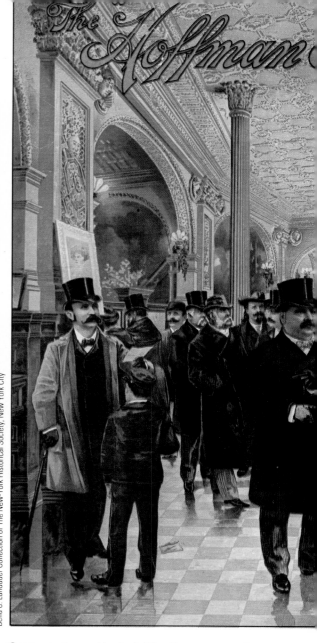

The constant round of receptions and formal dinners on tour exhausted the naturally shy Tchaikovsky. And although he was both touched and impressed by the warm genuine nature of American hospitality, thoughts of home were never far from his mind.

They then set off down Broadway, where Tchaikovsky bought himself a hat and some cigarettes. After a brief rest, courtesy visits were resumed; one of them was to Andrew Carnegie himself. Tchaikovsky rather liked the famous millionaire, largely, it seems, because Carnegie had an affection for Moscow. 'His wife is young and extremely sweet.' Home by eleven, after a visit to the Athletics Club, he fell into bed completely exhausted.

This was to be the pattern of the days that followed. Tchaikovsky was neither the first nor the last to find that the warmth of American hospitality could be overwhelming in all senses but, though struggling with his natural shyness and home-sickness, he was touched by the attentions paid him. At a formal dinner at Reno's:

Each lady also had my picture in a pretty frame. The dinner started at half-past seven and finished at eleven . . . Half-way through, an ice cream was served in some kinds of little boxes to which were attached small slates, with pencils and sponges, on which excerpts from my works were written in pencil. I then had to autograph the slates.

Dying for a cigarette, he managed to make his excuses at eleven, and half an hour later was on his way back to his hotel.

A triumphant reception

After further rehearsals at the Music Hall, interspersed with shopping, visits and sight-seeing, the day of the concert arrived: 5 May. The proceedings opened with massed singing of the Old Hundredth, *All people that on earth do dwell;* Reno then made a speech which (Tchaikovsky noted with sympathy) had been causing him considerable nerves. The national anthem *My country 'tis of thee* was sung, after which 'a clergyman made a long, and they say very boring, speech eulogizing the founders of the Hall and

Carnegie in particular'. The *Leonore* no. 3 overture brought them to the first interval. After it, Tchaikovsky conducted his Coronation March, 'with the authoritative strength of a master', the *Herald* noted next day.

Reading this review, Tchaikovsky found his gratification immediately followed by irritation at seeing himself described as nearly 60, embarrassed, and responding to the applause with a series of 'brusque and jerky bows'. Having his shyness remarked upon in print did nothing to bolster his confidence for the second concert, at which he was to conduct the Third Suite; but he was applauded wildly by the orchestra at the rehearsal, and managed to create a sensation at the concert. It was his 51st birthday: after the concert, he treated himself to a quiet walk, incognito, a solitary meal in a café and an early bed.

But now, in the wake of this triumph, the number of visitors and demands on his time was redoubled. He was plagued by persistent reporters; in the queue at his door were composers, autograph hunters, and an old man with a libretto for him to set. It was typical of Tchaikovsky that he gave most time to the last; he listened sympathetically to a tale of woe about the loss of the old man's only son, preferring his company to that of the predatory reporters. He also grew irritated with Damrosch, whom he found to be taking more than his share of rehearsal time –

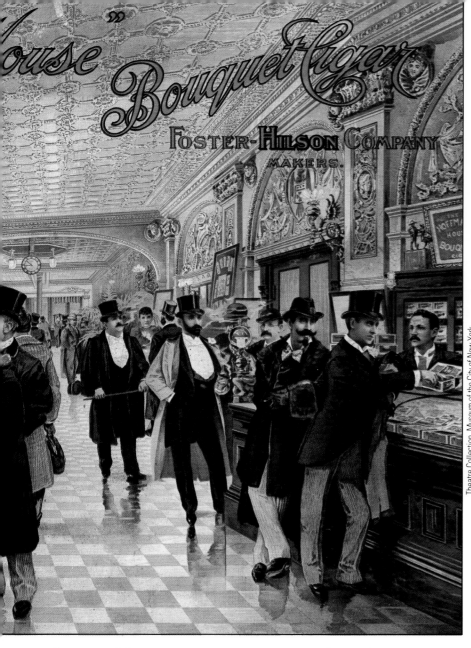

Tchaikovsky was a heavy smoker and often slipped out at night looking for somewhere to buy cigarettes. He frequented the fashionable Hoffman House hotel bar shown in this cigar advertisement (left).

an ancient complaint among musicians, but one which Tchaikovsky had perhaps the right to make. The work in hand was the First Piano Concerto:

It went beautifully in the excellent performance of the soloist Adele aus der Ohe. The enthusiasm was such as I never succeeded in arousing even in Russia. They called me out endlessly, shouting 'Upwards' and waved their handkerchieves – in a word, it was clear that I had really pleased the Americans. But especially dear to me was the enthusiasm of the orchestra.

Intermittent homesickness

The final concert of the festival included none of Tchaikovsky's own music; instead, it was given over to a performance of Handel's *Israel in Egypt*. Tchaikovsky noted this in his diary laconically, adding merely that the performance was very distinguished. The party that followed broke up finally at two in the morning, leaving Tchaikovsky in no state to cope with a day of visitors, hectic even by the standards he had grown used to. It was a Sunday, and his morning was filled with a stream of visitors who drove him, he wrote, 'to insensibility'. Some relief came with lunch with a Russian doctor, whose homesickness Tchaikovsky found more sympathetic than his Georgian princess wife. He stayed gossiping till

three, when he tore himself away to pay various duty calls. Suddenly, recalling that he was due at Carnegie's for dinner, he set off through the streets. Everything was shut, including the cafés: 'as they are the only places where 1) one may buy cigarettes and 2) satisfy Nature's little need, and I being in extreme want of both, one may imagine how great were my sufferings until I reached home.' His further indignation at the impossibility of buying a drink on a Sunday in New York was soothed by Carnegie's hospitality, and no less by Carnegie himself.

Tchaikovsky was filled with admiration for this simple, unaffected man who had acquired great wealth and used so much of it for philanthropic purposes; and the respect was cordially returned. Carnegie grasped Tchaikovsky warmly by the hands, and declared that he was the uncrowned king of music, embracing the amused composer and expressing the size of his talent by standing on tiptoe and throwing his arms on high. He then went into an imitation of Tchaikovsky conducting. After the embarrassment he had suffered at the hands of the press, Tchaikovsky might well have been upset: it is a measure of his liking for Carnegie that he found the imitation both accurate and funny.

On 11 May and 12 May there was a trip to Niagara Falls. With his Russian appreciation, of railways, Tchaikovsky described in considerable

The opening of the New York Music Hall (top) on 6 May 1891 was celebrated with a series of concerts at which Tchaikovsky was guest conductor. A founder of the Music Hall was the colourful millionaire Andrew Carnegie (above) whose humour – even when directed against the composer – Tchaikovsky particularly enjoyed.

Even in the 1890s a visit to the Niagara Falls (left) via the famous suspension bridge was a popular and well-advertised tourist attraction (above). Tchaikovsky took a two-day trip there and was so overawed by the Falls that he hardly knew what to say, though he did note his disappointment at not even being allowed to pick a dandelion as a memento. He was also impressed with the interiors of the American trains (right) with their luxurious furnishings and elaborate fittings.

The Capitol (right) was one of the sightseeing highlights for Tchaikovsky when, at the Russian Ambassador's invitation, he visited Washington. He wrote of the rich foliage surrounding the building and the breathtaking view of the city that stretched away from it.

detail the 'drawing room car', its attendants and the luxury of the surroundings. He was particularly impressed by the presence of a bathroom and a barber, although he seems to have patronized neither. He was lodged in a small hotel in Buffalo that reminded him of Switzerland, and to his pleasure he found the guests chiefly spoke German. The next morning saw him driving to the Falls, which astonished him beyond description.

That evening he set off again for New York, lying awake in his Pullman tormented by anxieties about the strains and stresses of the coming week.

Back at the Normandie, he was shocked to learn of the news from home of the attempt on the life of the future Nicholas II and depressed that there were no letters for him. Homesickness was intensified by saying goodbye to Damrosch, who was leaving for Europe; and further when he went to visit Ferdinand Mayer's summer home outside New York.

I felt so tired, irritated and unhappy that I could hardly keep from crying. Mayer's house and the neighbouring houses remind me very much of the dachas near Moscow in style. The only difference is that near Moscow there are groves, grass and flowers; here there is nothing but sand.

Centre of controversy

He returned to New York next day to find controversy surrounding a misunderstanding over Wagner. He had left the Music Hall after conducting his own Piano Concerto, exhausted and perspiring, and had thus missed the excerpts of Wagner's *Parsifal* that concluded the concert. This was interpreted as a gesture of disapproval of Wagner; and although Tchaikovsky was indeed no Wagnerian – his reports of the first Bayreuth Festival in 1876 are distinctly cool in tone – he did not lack respect for Wagner and did not in any case wish to make any particular point about Wagner's music on such an occasion. He wrote, in the *New York Morning Journal,* an article arguing that Wagner was, in his view, greater as a symphonic composer than as a strictly operatic composer. His point was misunderstood, and a week later the distinguished Wagner conductor Anton Seidl replied with 'A Defense of Wagner', suggesting that Tchaikovsky had completely failed to understand 'the music of the future'. The tone of Seidl's article was perfectly courteous, but the town scented controversy, and Tchaikovsky returned to New York to find a Miss Ivy Rose from the paper wanting a reply, which he attempted to write.

Further embarrassment came when Mayer sent a letter asking him to sign a testimonial for the Knabe pianos. Tchaikovsky seems to have agreed earlier to do this; but he was dismayed to find that the form of words drawn up for him to sign declared that they were indisputably the best in America. Though he liked the Knabe pianos well enough, he privately thought Steinways better (while disliking their representative). He extricated himself from this awkward situation by frankly telling Mayer that he really could not tell a lie and by seeking to find some other form of wording.

Baltimore and Philadelphia

Hardly had he settled back in New York, however, than he was obliged to pack his bags again. One of the conditions of his trip had been that he should visit Baltimore and Philadelphia, and his pleas on arrival that he should be let off were refused by Reno. He spent the night in his clothes on the train, and arrived in no very good temper to find his hotel indifferent, English the only language spoken, and the waiters reluctant to let him have the cup of tea with bread and butter which was all he wanted.

He was somewhat cheered by the arrival of Adele aus der Ohe, but spirits sank again when he reached the Lyceum Theatre and discovered that the orchestra was minute, with only four first violins, and under-rehearsed. He immediately abandoned the Third Suite in favour of the Serenade for Strings, which the orchestra's 40 players were just about able to manage; surprisingly, they seem to have made something of the Piano Concerto. Tchaikovsky did acknowledge that conditions were against them, for they were not a local group but the Boston Festival Orchestra, conducted by Victor Herbert, and they were exhausted by their travels at the end of a long season. He survived a long reception afterwards by drinking a good deal, and slept soundly.

However, he liked Baltimore. It was, he thought, 'a pretty, neat city'. He admired the Knabe piano factory, and took delight in the view of the harbour and in the architecture, especially the Peabody Insititute, whose facilities impressed him. He was sorry to have to move on to Philadelphia, though he found it 'very charming, all drowned in luxuriant spring verdure'. But to his dismay, as he embraced his host, a loose front tooth fell out, and could not be replaced. The nuisance of this was given an extra twist when he found that the accident made him whistle as he spoke; and at dinner that evening, among Russian speakers, he could not make sufficient distinction between 's', 'sh' and 'shch' – each of these sounds being a separate letter in Russian, and the subtle distinction between them being part of the music of the language. 'They all whistle like an old man', he confided sadly to his diary. However, he was cheered by the news that the Russian ambassador had returned specially to greet his eminent countryman, and that there was to be a reception at the Russian Embassy in Washington. There was a

After the frenetic pace of his triumphant American tour, Tchaikovsky was delighted to settle into the peace of his beloved Russian countryside (top). At long last he was able to progress with The Nutcracker. *A chance discovery of the previously unknown instrument, the celesta, provided him with the solution to the setting of the Sugar Plum fairy and he completed the score (title-page above) by April 1892.*

recital consisting of Brahms's First Piano Quartet and Tchaikovsky's own Piano Trio, the latter very well played by Hansen, the Secretary of the Embassy. They sat up talking and drinking until three, by which time most of the guests had gone.

After some more sight-seeing – Tchaikovsky was greatly impressed with the Capitol and 'the dense, luxuriant foliage of chestnut, acacia, oak and maple trees' – he spent some happy hours playing duets with Hansen before another evening concert. He stayed another night, once more enjoying Russian conviviality, before leaving for Philadelphia. He knew, however, that there was no need for rehearsal for his concert in this city, since it was a repeat with the Boston orchestra of the concert he had already given in Baltimore. It was indeed a success, with the Academy of Music crammed and the audience vociferous in their enthusiasm. A day later, after a dull journey, he was once more back in New York.

Fond farewells

By now he was growing obsessed with thoughts of home. Farewells were made to those who had been kind to him and had organized all his arrangements; he also found time to see once more the old librettist who had called on him previously, and told him gently that he could not write his opera. There were the final arrangements for the evening chamber concert of his music (a bad pianist 'who could not even count'); no less exhausting were the visits from people he scarcely knew who piled him high with gifts. At the concert, he replied to the ovation in French, which won him not only a further ovation but a bouquet of flowers flung into his face by a lady with more enthusiasm than aim.

Back at the hotel, he packed and retired, and was up again almost immediately to reach the boat by five o'clock in the morning, the sailing time. He was seen off by Reno and Mayer, over a couple of bottles of champagne. He fell into a light sleep, rousing himself only to come on deck in time to see the Statue of Liberty slipping astern. Earlier, he had been given a replica of the statue, but had ruefully abandoned it as he felt he would never get it past the Russian customs.

For the first time for weeks, on the journey home, Tchaikovsky took up composition again, making some sketches for a symphony. The trip had completely prevented work, but for all his complaints he does not seem to have regretted it. His descriptions of America, even though they are almost entirely of a few cities, are vivid and filled with lively touches of humour. He clearly liked Americans for their openness and warmth, their generosity and enthusiasm; he was less delighted by some of the importunities that went with this, especially as far as the press was concerned. Essentially a private man, he was able at times to take refuge from loneliness in the hospitality provided, and seems to have enjoyed receptions at which he could assume a public face more than dinner parties when he might be drawn into conversations against his will or be trapped by a bore: he met his share of the gushing American hostess on his travels.

But the impressions he carried away were not unfriendly, and for many of the difficulties he encountered he seems to have blamed himself, as much as anyone. Like Dvořák, he responded to the energy and excitement of the New World; and if he did not feel, like Dvořák, moved to make a musical response, his experience was enriched and his creative energies given new impetus. As soon as he reached home, with the greatest delight at being once more in his own countryside, he plunged back into *The Nutcracker*. For, on the way back through Paris, he had come across the then unknown instrument, the celesta, so the problem about how to set the Sugar Plum Fairy to music was resolved. Now his ideas came flowing back in full profusion.

'Pernicious passions'

Although Tchaikovsky's homosexuality was a cause of deep anguish and guilt throughout his life, it widened his understanding of human suffering and added a further dimension to his music.

Tchaikovsky grew up in a comfortable middle-class home. Like Mrs Hicks with her daughters and son (with book) in the painting below, the composer's mother was the central, home-making 'angel in the house'.

As a boy, Pyotr Tchaikovsky was unusually sensitive: as a man, his nerves were so tender that the merest thought of crowds could bring tears brimming to his eyes. He would tremble at the prospect of meeting people. He could be crushed by the violence of his response to a Mozart aria. Even parting from his family could drive him to despair. Yet, worst of all perhaps, was the burden of his homosexuality, a burden that caused him such deep anguish that he may eventually have taken his own life.

That Tchaikovsky's personal suffering profoundly influenced his music, there can be no doubt. His music is always deeply emotional, often extravagantly so, and occasionally it seems almost to drown in a morass of indulgent romantic fantasy – the kind of sentiment that meant Tchaikovsky was long dismissed by serious critics, though not the public, as a mere tearjerker. But it is impossible to listen to such a piece of music as the 'Pathétique' Symphony (no. 6) without feeling the real intensity of the composer's desolation. Much of Tchaikovsky's music is deeply neurotic, but also deeply affecting. It is, as Harold Schonberg suggests, as 'emotional as a scream from a window on a dark night'.

Fanny Durbach (left) was the much-loved governess of the Tchaikovsky family. Pyotr was deeply distressed when she was dismissed in 1848.

In 1893 Tchaikovsky (below) received an honorary degree at Cambridge. If his homosexuality had been known, such a public image would have been shattered.

Novosti

Novosti

The 'oldest profession' enjoyed something of a heyday in Tchaikovsky's time. For all its starchiness, the prevailing moral code made room for sleazy salons (below) and street-walking prostitutes (left), but made no such open provision for homosexuals.

The pain that inflamed Tchaikovsky's music seems almost to be the driving force behind it. The pent-up emotional need, frustrated elsewhere, burst out with vivid intensity in his music. Music provided a bottomless chalice into which he could pour a flood of passion that could not be released in close personal relationships.

Fear and guilt

For many years, the root of Tchaikovsky's emotional problems remained hidden from the world, known only to the composer's closest friends, though, of course, rumours often got out. Throughout his life, Tchaikovsky lived in constant fear that his homosexuality would be discovered. After his death, his younger brother Modest, also homosexual, destroyed many of the most revealing records – diary entries and letters to friends and relatives – and the real extent of Tchaikovsky's sexual activities remains unknown even today.

That Tchaikovsky should fear exposure so much is, to say the least, understandable. If today homosexuals are still regarded with suspicion by some, in 19th-century Russia they could be regarded with abhorrence. In an age when sex between married men and women was sometimes considered a necessary evil, few people would openly acknowledge the existence of homosexuality. None would condone it. Anyone whose homosexuality became public knowledge faced complete social rejection. Worse still, for a composer like Tchaikovsky, exposure carried the fear not only of being cut off from personal relationships, but also that his music, his one outlet, would become impossible, since no respectable musician would touch his compositions.

cannot mention it in terms other than 'this' or 'Z'. His burden of guilt was sometimes agonizing – and it was possibly this extreme guilt, more than anything, that prevented him finding fulfilment even in relationships with men.

'A porcelain child'

Tchaikovsky's emotional insecurity is evident right from his early childhood. Fanny Durbach, the governess young Pyotr loved so dearly, described him as 'a porcelain child', beautiful but terribly delicate emotionally.

On the whole, Pyotr was a happy child, an open, affectionate boy who, as Fanny said, 'you could not help loving . . . because he loved everybody'. But he was hypersensitive and deeply wounded by the most trivial upset. The mildest reproof would be etched sharply in his mind and gave him such anguish that hours, even days, after the event, he would suddenly dissolve in tears.

Fanny was very much a surrogate mother in Pyotr's early years and he was passionately devoted to her. He was completely distraught when she stayed behind in Votkinsk as the Tchaikovsky family moved to Moscow in 1848. A full year later, a letter from his beloved Fanny still upset him deeply.

In Moscow, Pyotr's emotional dependence devolved on his mother and his love for her became almost obsessive. Some have suggested that it is in his anguished devotion, first to Fanny and then to his mother, that the seeds of Tchaikovsky's latent homosexuality were sown. In his biography of the composer, Herbert Weinstock says that Pyotr's love for his mother 'had all the intensity of a lover's passion' and is certain that in their relationship lay the prime cause of Tchaikovsky's homosexuality.

Whether or not we agree with this interpretation, it is clear that Pyotr's unusually intense dependence on his mother – and also the security of the family home – foreshadowed problems to come. The parting from his mother when he was sent to school in St Petersburg was devastating and he always remembered it as one of the most terrible days of his life. As his mother tried to board the coach back to Moscow, Pyotr clung to her so desperately that he had to be torn away forcibly, and, as her coach moved off, he lunged after it, grabbing desperately at the footboard and anything he could reach, crying in anguish as it gradually left him behind.

The enforced separation from his family was hardly bearable for the nine year-old Tchaikovsky, and his letters home from school are pathetic in their frantic expressions of love. Often he calls his parents 'my beautiful angels' and begs them to come and see him. Memories of home always brought him to tears. It was the security and warmth of the family home that he missed as much as his mother and he was never happier than when the family came to St Petersburg at last, and he was able to spend the summer with Nikolay, Sasha, Polya, Malya, Katya and Mina. Yet, unable to marry successfully, Tchaikovsky as an adult was never again to have the security of family life that he so badly needed – only the home of his sister Sasha and her husband in Kamenka would provide a refuge in years to come.

Undoubtedly, the death of his beloved mother in 1854 was a terrible blow for Tchaikovsky, more terrible than that first parting. Yet, safe in the family home, Tchaikovsky was able to cope with the loss and the signs of emotional stress seemed to submerge for many years. But he began to turn, as he

A Victorian husband (above) discovers his 'erring wife's' infidelity, and her utter ruin is nigh. Like Tchaikovsky's unfortunate wife, she is now an outcast from respectable society.

But it was not only the fear of exposure that caused Tchaikovsky pain. Although a remarkably thoughtful and perceptive man, his background was very conventional and he too, like the people around him, felt that homosexuality was wrong and unnatural. He was beset with an immeasurable sense of guilt and, for many years, he tried to fight against his secret 'vice', believing it a sin and a disease. In his diaries, in one of the few references left, he calls himself 'a monster' – an immensely poignant comment in the light of the sensitivity and consideration for others which shine through in his letters.

Tchaikovsky was never less than honest with himself and though he believed – like many of his contemporaries – that homosexuality was a sickness that could be cured, he never tried to deny his own true nature to himself. Yet his distaste for his problem was profound and even in his diaries he had always done, to music as a solace for his grief. He started thinking seriously about composition for the first time. In July 1854, less than a month after his mother's death, he started work on a one-act opera to be called *Hyperbole,* suggested by his stepsister Zinaida's brother-in-law Viktor Olkhovsky. This work never came to much, but a month later he had completed the *Anastasie Valse.* All his life, Tchaikovsky was to turn to music in moments of pain, and some of his most creative phases stemmed from times of depression.

'Contemptible rumours'

Nevertheless, Tchaikovsky's time at the St Petersburg School of Jurisprudence was not an altogether unhappy one. And, if his homosexual inclinations had begun to emerge, they seemed not to provoke the anxiety they were later to do. Isolated from girls, many of Tchaikovsky's contemporaries at boys' boarding schools received their

Nobles celebrate the coronation in 1881 (right) of Tsar Alexander III who honoured Tchaikovsky with the Order of St Vladimir. This gesture moved the composer all the more deeply because of his personal insecurity.

'Artistic' photos of classically-garbed Italian boys (far right) had an established homosexual audience in 19th-century Europe.

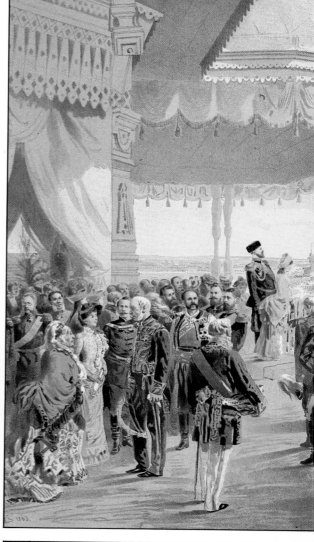

sexual initiation with other boys — helped along by the rituals of beatings and fagging — and the School of Jurisprudence was well known at the time for homosexual activity. Most boys went on to form normal relationships with women in later life and it is unlikely that Tchaikovsky was unduly anxious that any bias towards men would last beyond school — though even at the tender age of 14, he was smoking to calm his nerves, and eventually became totally addicted.

When Tchaikovsky joined the Ministry of Justice after graduation in 1859, he began to develop close friendships with young men such as Alexey Apukhtin, who joined him for daily poetry sessions. But his sexual inclinations still do not seem to have caused him concern and his comments to his sister and confidante Sasha that 'contemptible rumours' were circulating about him suggest that these relationships may have been genuinely platonic. Indeed, he was quite the young dandy, and even dallied lightly with young ladies, though never expressing a real interest.

In summer 1861, Tchaikovsky embarked on the first of many trips to western Europe. Trips like these afforded an opportunity for him to be together with men, away from the eyes of rumour and in a climate less unfavourable to homosexuals. In Paris and

Young graduates from the School of Jurisprudence (above), which Tchaikovsky attended. At schools such as this the so-called 'double standard', whereby men lived according to a separate moral code, was learned. The duel (right), like exclusively male clubs, was an aspect of this masculine culture. Escorted by their seconds, the duellists would settle — not necessarily fatally — an 'affair of honour'.

Novosti

love with a woman. Only when he graduated from the Conservatoire at the end of 1865 did his troubles really begin.

Growing problems

First of all, he began to suffer from bouts of acute depression in which he felt completely isolated, declaring that he had a 'hatred of the human race'. Moving to Moscow to take up the job with the eminent musician Nikolay Rubinstein was a terrible experience for him, for it meant leaving behind his family and friends. He missed the twins sorely.

As Tchaikovsky began to work on his First Symphony, these fits of depression began to become more and more acute. He spent the summer with the Davidovs, the family of Sasha's husband, and worked

feverishly to finish the symphony, often labouring deep into the night. But the strain began to tell and in August he started hallucinating and found his hands and feet going numb. Soon he suffered a complete nervous collapse and the doctor was called in to find him 'one step away from insanity'.

At the same time, a series of encounters began to plant doubt in Tchaikovsky's mind, doubt that he would ever be able to form a relationship with a woman. It may be this dawning knowledge that made the fits so severe. The first encounter, in February 1866, was with a girl called Mufka Tarnovsky. Tchaikovsky found her very attractive and was ready to start an affair, but within weeks realized he had no real feelings for her. Then, in the summer, there was Vera Davidova.

Vera was Sasha's sister-in-law and the Davidov family very much hoped that she and Tchaikovsky would get married. Indeed, it is probable that the composer was invited to spend the summer with the Davidovs specifically to further the match.

Vera was very attracted to Tchaikovsky and the composer was very fond of her and greatly admired her. But for Tchaikovsky there was nothing more. Sexually, she left him cold. It was perhaps his frustration at remaining unaroused that drove him to the frenzied nocturnal labour on the First Symphony

Vienna, at least – unlike Russia – homosexuality was not illegal in private, though it was still morally condemned. In the future, the composer was often to take advantage of this freedom, sometimes with lovers, sometimes just with friends and fellow musicians. But this first trip, with one Vasily Pisarev, upset him badly. He returned cursing Pisarev as 'incredibly base' with 'the most vile qualities of mind' and it seems likely that Pisarev had made some kind of homosexual overtures. It may be that Tchaikovsky still rejected the idea of homosexual involvement altogether; it may just be that Pisarev offended the sense of delicacy that pervaded the composer's later relationships with men. Interestingly, it was at this time that a strong bond began to develop between Tchaikovsky and his young twin brothers Modest and Anatoly. He felt very protective towards the twins and often tried to replace the mother they had lost at the age of four.

On his return from the trip with Pisarev, Tchaikovsky began to take up music seriously, going for lessons with Zaremba and later enrolling at the St Petersburg Conservatoire. He always regarded this as the happiest period of his life. As he threw himself enthusiastically into his music, he acquired a circle of close and much-loved men friends, but seemed to remain convinced that he would eventually fall in that had brought on his nervous breakdown.

Over the next few years, Vera was to cause Tchaikovsky a great deal of pain – Vera was deeply wounded too. Fond of her and, no doubt, hoping that he might fall in love, Tchaikovsky did not discourage her as strongly as he might have done. While she became more and more deeply involved, he, to his deep anguish, remained uninterested. In his biography of the composer, David Brown quotes a letter to Sasha of 28 April 1868:

The one thing that torments and frightens me is Vera. Tell me: what should I do ... I feel that I would conceive a hatred for her if the question of fulfilling our relationship in marriage should become serious ... There are no beings as wonderful as she is. But I am so base and ungrateful that I cannot act as I should, and I am terribly tormented. Help me set my mind at rest – and for God's sake, tear up this letter.

Probably to get away from Vera, Tchaikovsky accepted an offer to go on another trip, this time with Vladimir Shilovsky. Shilovsky was yet another of the men in the composer's life and Tchaikovsky would often spend quiet summer weeks at Shilovsky's farm – though, of course, it is impossible to tell what kind of relationship they had. During this European trip, Tchaikovsky completed his first major opera, *The Voyevoda,* which was performed at the Bolshoy in Moscow on 11 February 1869.

In his sensational novel, **Against Nature** *(1884), the French writer Georges Huysmans (left) created a decadent and morally ambiguous hero who was much admired by Oscar Wilde and his set. Tchaikovsky, however, always a rather conservative individual, would have recoiled from the flamboyant tastes of these writers.*

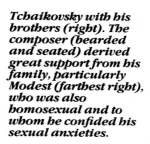

The Yellow Book, *a periodical of the 1890s, boasted bold and risqué illustrations (left) by Aubrey Beardsley. Oscar Wilde, a contributor to* The Yellow Book, *was pilloried when his homosexuality was made public and the periodical became a casualty of the scandal. The knife-edge existence of homosexuals who were also celebrities was all too familiar to Tchaikovsky.*

Tchaikovsky with his brothers (right). The composer (bearded and seated) derived great support from his family, particularly Modest (farthest right), who was also homosexual and to whom he confided his sexual anxieties.

Oscar Wilde (above). Despite his popularity and fame as a writer, prosecution as a homosexual in 1895 (two years after Tchaikovsky's death) was his ruin.

Ideal heroines and real women

It was during the rehearsals for *The Voyevoda* that Tchaikovsky became involved with the opera singer Desirée Artôt – quickly taking the relationship to the point where marriage was on the cards. Coming so soon after the anguish over Vera, the affair is a little strange, and always seems to have had a slightly whimsical nature. Although Tchaikovsky found the real Desirée a 'nice, good, sensible woman', perhaps the attraction was based on the romantic ideal of Artôt the artist rather than genuine desire. Either way, he did not seem unduly upset when she suddenly married the Spanish baritone Mariano Padilla.

It was gradually becoming clear that if Tchaikovsky remained attracted to the idea of involvement with women, his desire evaporated in practice. More and more, he seems to have indulged in romantic fantasies, creating ideal heroines in his music and then falling in love with them. A vein of lush romanticism runs right through Tchaikovsky's compositions. Ballets like *Swan Lake* rival *Romeo and Juliet* in the public imagination as perfect expressions of romantic heterosexual love. That these romances should be created by a confirmed homosexual seems strange until you realize that in his music, perhaps, Tchaikovsky was able to fulfil a yearning frustrated in life.

For ten years, Tchaikovsky gave up the idea of marriage, but his loneliness and desperate need for emotional security seemed only to be exacerbated by a series of affairs with men and a succession of trips to western Europe. Among the possible lovers was the French composer Camille Saint-Saëns who came to Moscow in 1875. The two musicians were immediately attracted, but the cordiality soon chilled and, if Tchaikovsky entertained any hopes of a lasting friendship, they were quickly dashed.

During the 1870s, Tchaikovsky's bouts of depression became more and more frequent, and his feelings of isolation became more and more profound. His disgust with his vices became acute and he threw himself feverishly into composition, writing many piano pieces and songs between 1874 and 1876. In September 1876, Tchaikovsky wrote to Modest that he had decided the only way out of his problems was to marry, both to rid himself of his 'pernicious passions' and 'habits' and because they were causing so much pain to his loved ones.

Nothing was to come of this resolution immediately and the next year he started up his long relationship with Nadezhda von Meck. This bizarre relationship is open to many interpretations, but it is possible that it provided Tchaikovsky's ideal liaison with a woman – by never meeting her he was never confronted with the problem of lack of physical attraction. Yet this liaison, if it was satisfying in many ways, did nothing for his respectability and when, in the midst of another bout of depression, he received an ardent letter from a female admirer, Antonina Milyukova, he embarked on a course that proved to be truly disastrous – marriage.

Within hours he realized he found Antonina repugnant. Within weeks, he tried to escape by standing in an icy river to bring on pneumonia. The doctor recommended immediate separation and Anatoly took him away to western Europe, but the pain of that awful mistake lingered on for many years.

Music as a refuge

Again, music was to be his refuge and in Venice later that year, Tchaikovsky worked obsessively on the completion of the Fourth Symphony. In this symphony, perhaps for the first time, Tchaikovsky used his music to express his emotional turmoil and if the effect if not quite so stunning as later works in this vein, such as the *Manfred* Symphony and the *Pathétique,* the piece is still impressive. The Symphony was, wrote Tchaikovsky, 'an echo of what I was going through at the time'.

Although he continued to compose works in an idealistic vein, the element of personal expression became more and more important, giving his music a power and scope it had lacked before. There were bad patches, of course, but over the next 15 years of his life, masterpieces began to flow from his pen and if his loneliness continued to torture him, it seemed to do his music good, not harm.

Tchaikovsky's emotional involvement in his music culminated in the last year of his life in the magnificent and deeply moving Pathétique Symphony (no. 6), composed in 1893. It was, as Tchaikovsky declared, 'subjective to the core', a programme symphony with a theme so poignant and painful that he often wept bitterly while composing it: the final movement is a desolate cry from the heart. It was the last music Tchaikovsky ever wrote. Within a week of the première he was dead, perhaps from cholera, perhaps by committing suicide to avoid the humiliation and pain of exposure as a homosexual.

COMPOSER'S LIFE

Madame Nadezhda von Meck

Tchaikovsky hated his homosexuality, believing that it prevented his happiness since he had to live with the constant fear of discovery and the resulting scandal that would destroy him. In the hope of living what he saw as a normal life, Tchaikovsky married in 1877 but the marriage was a disaster and at one point threatened, he thought, to drive him mad. He found a much more satisfactory relationship with a woman in his correspondence with a rich widow, Nadezhda von Meck, whom he never met although she and Tchaikovsky exchanged letters for 13 years. She supported him with money, which allowed him to work free of the burden of financial insecurity, but the emotional and spiritual relationship between them was more important to Tchaikovsky and he was greatly grieved when Madame von Meck suddenly broke off the correspondence.

'My dear best friend'

For 13 years – until a sad and sudden estrangement – Tchaikovsky was supported financially and emotionally by the reclusive widow Nadezhda von Meck. They exchanged over 1100 letters, but never spoke.

1877 was a momentous year for Pyotr Il'yich Tchaikovsky. At the age of 37 he came into contact with two women who were to have a profound effect on his life – the one brought him to the brink of disaster; the other was his salvation. The first he married; the second he met only by accident and never spoke to. The circumstances of his life were such that he needed both of them desperately.

Tchaikovsky had strong emotional ties with his family in St Petersburg but he was living far away from them in Moscow. He was still struggling to make ends meet – and still a teacher, albeit at the august Moscow Conservatory. This institution was under the directorship of the formidable Nikolay Rubinstein, one of the most brilliant virtuosi of the day. Tchaikovsky's relationship with his employer was fraught. Rubinstein recognized his genius but was cruelly destructive in criticizing his music.

There was a further problem. Tchaikovsky's homosexuality filled him with self-loathing. He saw his 'vice' as an obstacle to his happiness and lived in fear of discovery and a scandal that would ruin his reputation as a man and his prospects as a composer.

In order to compose he needed security, both financial and emotional. In 1876 he thought he had discovered how to come by both at once when he resolved to make a serious effort to marry. But this decision was a desperate one and he dreaded the prospect.

The other woman

As Tchaikovsky braced himself for the horrors of matrimony another woman stole almost imperceptibly into his life. Nadezhda von Meck was a wealthy widow of 46, a recluse and the owner of various estates including a house in Moscow's fashionable Rodeztvensky Boulevard, where she lived in splendour among seven of her twelve children and a retinue of servants. One source claims that her husband, whose fortune had been made by her

Tchaikovsky (above) was a moody, emotionally unstable man, shattered by his mother's death when he was 14, and almost destroyed by a disastrous marriage to one of his former students. He found comfort and true friendship in Nadezhda von Meck (above left) whom he occasionally addressed as 'my dear best friend'. Introduced to Tchaikovsky's music by his teacher Nikolay Rubinstein, von Meck wrote at once to the composer. Their correspondence quickly developed; the letter (left) – one of more than 1100 that passed between them — was written by Tchaikovsky in 1878, after he had agreed to accept financial support from her – support which was invaluable.

The wealthy von Meck family circle (left). Karl von Meck (centre left), Nadezhda's husband, who had made a small fortune by investing wisely in the railways, purportedly died of a heart attack on hearing of his wife's infidelity. Nadezhda had an affair with his engineer (back row second from left) by whom she had had an illegitimate daughter (shown seated on her lap). The child later married a nobleman who, on discovering the affair, blackmailed Nadezhda for the rest of her life.

business acumen, had died of a heart attack on being told of her infidelity. Perhaps this was why, in her widowhood, music became her solace.

Nikolay Rubinstein was one of the rare visitors to Nadezhda's house and he first introduced her to Tchaikovsky's work. Describing his employee as a struggling musician, he gave her a copy of *The Tempest*. She was so overwhelmed on playing it through that she described herself as 'half-demented'.

Nadezhda commissioned an arrangement from Tchaikovsky and her letter of thanks for the work set the tone for the correspondence that was to follow:

To tell you into what ecstasies your work sent me would be unfitting, since you are accustomed to praise and admiration from those much better qualified than a creature so musically insignificant as I. It would only make you laugh . . .

Such a letter was bound to find favour with a composer not altogether 'accustomed to praise and admiration'. He thanked her sincerely, writing that he was comforted to hear of the existence of a 'true and passionate music lover'.

Nadezhda followed up her second commission with a charmingly tentative invitation to friendship: 'I should like to tell you a great deal more about my feelings towards you but I am afraid of taking up your time, of which you have so little to spare.' Tchaikovsky encouraged her: 'It would have been very pleasant and interesting, for I, too, reciprocate your feelings.' Now the floodgates opened and letters were exchanged with

feverish haste – over the next 13 years they poured out their feelings about life, love, music, nature, philosophy and each other in more than 1100 letters.

A spiritual romance

Only two topics were taboo. Tchaikovsky's homosexuality was never mentioned, although some biographers believe Nadezhda must have known about it and understood that silence was necessary. The other subject that caused Tchaikovsky some embarrassment was money, but with the help of Nadezhda's tact and generosity he overcame his qualms and was able to ask her for a substantial loan as early as May 1877.

He had refused a third commission, knowing that she was offering it out of charity, because he 'could not bear any insincerity or falsehood to creep into our relationship'. But as a token of his gratitude for the money that arrived anyway, he dedicated his Fourth Symphony to her. Nadezhda was a happy benefactress:

*Why should you spoil my pleasure in taking care of
you . . . You hurt me. If I wanted something from you,
of course you would give it me – is it not so?
Very well, then we are quits. Do not interfere with
my management of your domestic economy, Pyotr
Il'yich.*

And she spared him any further embarrassment by granting him an annuity of 6,000 roubles besides numerous handsome presents, all of which enabled Tchaikovsky to live in comfort and to help his family.

This business-like arrangement meant that their spiritual romance could continue untainted by unpleasant essentials. Nadezhda expressed her fear of personal acquaintance:

*There was a time when I earnestly desired your
personal acquaintance: but now I feel the more you
fascinate me, the more I shrink from knowing you. It
seems to me that I could not then talk to you as I do
now . . . at present I prefer to think of you at a safe
distance and to be at one with you in your music.*

Tchaikovsky agreed, 'I feel that on close acquaintance you would not find that harmony between myself and my music, of which you have dreamed.'

Physical intimacy would have been impossible for Tchaikovsky; Nadezhda found a substitute for it in his music. Under the influence of his melodies she was liable to succumb to palpitations, breathlessness, weeping and even fainting. His music, she said, coursed like an electric shock through her veins. She also enjoyed her maternal role, for her protégé had suffered greatly when he lost his mother at the age of 14.

But although the relationship was mutually supportive and gave Tchaikovsky everything he needed from a woman, the fact that it was conducted from a distance and in secret (only his close family knew the extent and nature of his involvement with Nadezhda) meant that one thing was still lacking – the public respectability of matrimony.

Enter Antonina

In May 1877 help arrived in the form of a passionate love-letter from one of Tchaikovsky's students at the Conservatory, 20-year-old Antonina Milyukova. Tchaikovsky's cordial reply was followed by an invitation to visit the young lady. Tchaikovsky accepted. From letters written afterwards it would seem that during their meeting Antonina discovered that her love could never be returned, and Tchaikovsky discovered that Antonina was a person of

little intelligence with no musical interest or ability. But Antonina was determined. 'I cannot live without you,' she wrote, 'and so perhaps I shall soon put an end to my life.' This was one of a series of suicide threats that had a profound effect on Tchaikovsky. Later he wrote that this placed him in a painful dilemma: 'Either I must keep my freedom at the expense of this woman's ruin . . . or I must marry.'

He proposed to Antonina barely a month after they first met. The wedding date was set for 18 July, but Tchaikovsky was unable to pluck up the courage to write to Nadezhda until three days before the event. The marriage was already doomed and, obviously fearing that Nadezhda would feel betrayed, Tchaikovsky took great pains to make this clear.

*God knows I am filled with the best of intentions
towards the future companion of my life, and if we
are both unhappy I shall not be to blame. My
conscience is clear.*

'Ghastly spiritual torment'

Two days into the 'honeymoon', Tchaikovsky could contain his 'ghastly spiritual torment' no longer and began to pour out his sufferings in a series of agonized letters. He confessed that he found Antonina 'physically repulsive', but tried to calm himself: 'she will not really bother me' because 'she is very limited'. A faint hope. On their return to Moscow Tchaikovsky collapsed and feared himself on the brink of madness.

He had, however, reckoned without Nadezhda. Later she was able to tell him how she had really felt

Brailov (left) was Madame von Meck's country estate, where Tchaikovsky often went to rest. He would row across the lake and work undisturbed in the summer house. If Nadezhda was also in residence, elaborate precautions were taken to ensure they didn't meet. Despite this, Tchaikovsky's carriage one day met hers on a narrow path in the woods. Both were confused, and Tchaikovsky later wrote apologizing for the incident.

when he made his unfortunate marriage:

I am jealous . . . as a woman is jealous of the man she loves. Do you know, when you married, it was intensely difficult for me, as though some part of my heart had broken. The thought that you were near that woman was bitter and unbearable.

But the letter that was waiting for him after his honeymoon was one of congratulation. Tchaikovsky seized upon its friendly tone and wrote a frantic reply, begging for a loan of 1000 roubles, with which he could 'go away, far away, to be alone, to rest, to think things over, to be treated, and lastly to work'. The money was sent by return of post. 'Do you realise how wicked I am?' Nadezhda confessed two years after this episode:

I was glad when you were unhappy with her . . . I hated that woman because she did not make you happy, but I should have hated her a hundred times more if you had found happiness with her. I believed that she had robbed me of what should be mine alone, what is rightfully mine for the reason that I love you more than anyone and value you above anything else in the world.

Conscious only of the immense kindness of his benefactress and unaware that she had regarded the rescue as a personal triumph, Tchaikovsky gratefully confided in her from his retreat in Kiev. Nadezhda then learned of his abhorrence for Antonina, that he had become so distraught he thought he would never compose again and had even contemplated suicide.

But the retreat 'cure' lasted only until he returned to Moscow, where once again with Antonina, Tchaikovsky teetered on the edge of insanity. In October he walked fully clothed into the River Moskva and stood in its freezing waters waiting to catch pneumonia. When this failed he telegraphed his brother Anatol and got him to send an urgent 'official' message requesting his presence immediately in St Petersburg. Anatol obliged. Once there, Tchaikovsky collapsed and was unconscious for two days. The doctor prescribed 'a complete change of life and scene'.

Exit Antonina

The first and most essential measure was a divorce. Anatol travelled to Moscow with Nikolay Rubinstein and to their surprise Antonina agreed to the idea straight away. In practice, she was not so easily disposed of. The only ground for divorce in Russia at that time was adultery, and Antonina soon retracted her promise and refused to bring this charge against her husband. She wandered from lover to lover, periodically uttering threats and being paid off by Tchaikovsky's lawyers, who became so afraid that she might reveal his homosexuality in a scandalous court case that they eventually advised him no longer to sue for divorce – even when she bore an illegitimate child. In 1896, the hapless Antonina was finally certified insane and committed to an asylum.

Now that Tchaikovsky was free of the 'whirlpool of lies, pretence and hypocrisy', he went to Switzerland to recuperate and to work. Well pleased with the course of events, Nadezhda wrote soothing words to assuage his feelings of guilt towards Antonina:

You are not guilty of wronging her in any way, and you may be sure she will not suffer at all from the

separation. *[Antonina] is one of those fortunate ones who, because they lack education, never suffer deeply or for long since they cannot feel anything deeply... If someone tells you that she weeps, do not be disturbed: be sure she does it only for show.*

This was balm to Tchaikovsky's tortured nerves and he entered into the spirit of self-congratulation by reviling his hapless wife's empty heart and total ignorance of his music. But reason was returning and he did admit that Antonina had been utterly blameless for her part in the disastrous marriage.

Tchaikovsky now returned to his music. 'Every note that comes from my pen in the future will be dedicated to you', he wrote to Nadezhda. He kept her informed as to the progress of his composition and provided detailed and fascinating insights into his method of working. He describes the frenzied excitement of spontaneous composition and his fight against indolence and disinclination, discussing points of musical theory with her.

Since, to Nadezhda, the music was the embodiment of the man, reading about its composition brought him thrillingly near. Longing to share her life more intimately with him, she invited him in 1878 to Florence, where she had rented him an apartment. She herself was staying not far off, and, mindful of their agreement not to meet, she gave him a schedule of their daily walks so that their paths would not cross. Despite these elaborate precautions, they actually caught sight of each other several times, but acknowledged the encounter only by bowing. Not once did they speak.

The excitement was repeated when Tchaikovsky was invited to Nadezhda's country estate at Brailov and they met accidentally in the woods.

...t in the mountains of the ...aucasus, in the south of the ...ussian Empire, Tiflis (below) ...as Tchaikovsky's ideal ...treat. There, with his brother ...natol (who was Vice-...overnor) and his family, ...chaikovsky found peace after ...s exhausting European ...urs and the pressure of life ...1 Moscow and St Petersburg. ...was a cruel twist of fate that ...1 Tiflis, in 1890, he received ...om Madame von Meck the ...tter ending their ...lationship.

Although we were face to face for only a moment, I felt horribly confused. However, I raised my hat politely. She seemed to lose her head completely and did not know what to do.

The encounter stirred a different mixture of emotions in Nadezhda and her account sounded a particularly dangerous note:

Marcel André Baschet: Claude Debussy/Bulloz © DACS 1990

The French composer Claude Debussy (above) who was also taken under Mme von Meck's wing.

I felt so gay and happy that tears came to my eyes... I do not seek any close personal relationship with you, but I love to be near you passively, tacitly... To feel you, not as a myth, but as a living man whom I love sincerely.

When she went further in such 'unintentional confessions' Tchaikovsky promptly insisted that his love for her could be expressed only through his music. The relationship remained safely confined to the written word.

Exit Nadezhda

And so it continued, though the peak of intensity had passed, until 1890, when the correspondence ended abruptly and in a manner that shocked Tchaikovsky deeply. In October Nadezhda wrote that she was about to be declared bankrupt. Tchaikovsky's allowance was to be discontinued. 'Do not forget,' she ended her parting letter, 'and think of me sometimes.' Tchaikovsky was extremely shaken. Though welcome, the annuity was no longer crucial to his survival. But he could not bear to contemplate the end of their friendship and he wrote back immediately.

She never replied, though he wrote again and again. The only explanation for her sudden break with the composer is that offered by her granddaughter, Galina von Meck, who maintains that Nadezhda was suffering from an extreme nervous disorder as well as tuberculosis, and was too ill to write. Whatever the reason, Tchaikovsky never recovered and some say that it was Nadezhda that he cursed on his deathbed in November 1893. Nadezhda was to follow him to the grave three months later, taking the mystery with her.

Contemporary composers

Mily Balakirev (1837-1910)

Born in Gorky of a prosperous aristocratic family, Balakirev grew up in the country, where he heard the Russian peasant music that influenced his later music. Through a friend and neighbour who had a private orchestra, he became familiar with the standard classics of music, from Mozart to Liszt. In St Petersburg, he collected and edited folk songs, founding the Free School of Music which propounded strongly nationalistic musical doctrines. He was one of the group, 'The Five,' all of whom had similar aims. His most famous works are the symphonic poem *Taloney* (1867–82) and *Islamey,* both of which Liszt played. Balakirev died in St Petersburg.

Alexander Borodin (1833-87)

Borodin trained as a doctor and a professor of chemistry before he met Balakirev and became a member of the group called 'The Five'. Then, in his late twenties, he decided to devote himself to music but only in the spare time left by his profession. He wrote two symphonies and a symphonic sketch *In the Steppes of Central Asia,* three string quartets, songs, piano music and the opera *Prince Igor.* Borodin was not so melodramatically 'Russian' as some of his contemporaries, preferring boldly outlined melodies. He died suddenly at a party in St Petersburg.

Edvard Grieg (1843-1907)

Born in Bergen, Norway, in 1843, Grieg was the first Scandinavian composer to win universal acceptance abroad. At an early age he showed signs of his musical talent, studying first in Leipzig, Germany, and then in Copenhagen. Becoming aware of the riches of Norwegian folk music, he wrote the first version of the famed *Piano Concerto in A minor* in 1868, though later he revized it many times. In 1874 Ibsen invited him to compose incidental music for *Peer Gynt,* which has also achieved global recognition. He travelled widely, conducting his own music, England being the last country where he performed in 1906. He died in Bergen in 1907.

Modest Mussorgsky (1839-81)

Although born into a wealthy family, Mussorgsky was poor for much of his life, partly because his family lost money when the serfs were freed and partly because of his own mismanagement. Much of his music was unfinished at his death, but his opera, *Boris Gudonov,* and solo piano pieces, *Pictures from an Exhibition,* are superb examples of their genres. He never made music his full-time career, supporting himself with a minor civil service job. He died of alcoholic epilepsy in St Petersburg.

Nikolay Rimsky-Korsakov (1844-1908)

Born in Tikhvin in 1844, Rimsky-Korsakov was raised in the country like many of the Russian composers, so benefiting from childhood acquaintance with folk songs. While serving in the navy, he composed his first symphony in 1865, which gained him a professorial post at St. Petersburg Conservatory. He was very strongly nationalistic in his music, showing a dramatic sense of orchestral colour that anticipates Stravinsky. He wrote three symphonies, the suite *Sheherazade,* choral music and several operas, including *The Maid of Pskov, The Snow Maiden* and *The Golden Cockerel.* He died in Lyubensk.

Nikolay Rubinstein (1835-81)

Born in Moscow in 1835, Rubinstein achieved fame as a pianist and composer early in life and became a key figure in Moscow's musical life. In 1860 he founded the Moscow branch of the Russian Musical Society which turned into the Moscow Conservatory six years later, Rubinstein becoming its director until his death. A close friend of Tchaikovsky, he is best known for his initial dismissal of his First Piano Concerto as 'worthless and unplayable'. He later admitted he was mistaken and conducted the first Moscow performance of the Concerto and championed other contemporary composers. He died on a visit to Paris in 1881 after eating a dozen oysters in bed.

Alexander Skryabin (1872-1915)

Born in Moscow, Skryabin early showed remarkable musical talent, being able to play anything he heard on the piano by the age of six. He attended the Moscow Conservatory before being taken up by Belyayev, the patron-publisher of Russian music, who published his compositions as they were finished. Starting as an admirer and highly original imitator of Chopin, Skryabin gradually changed his harmonic idiom, coming to use many upward leaps in his rhythms. His later works, which include *The Divine Poem* and *The Poem of Fire,* are passionate and complex, showing signs of his mystical theories that linked aesthetics with religion and cosmogony. He died of a tumour in Moscow in 1915.

Bibliography

G. Abraham, *Tchaikovsky,* Hyperion Press, Westport, 1979

E. Blom, *Tchaikovsky: Orchestral Works,* Greenwood Press, Westport, 1927

D. Brown, *Tchaikovsky: The Early Years 1840-1874,* Norton Press, New York, 1979

D. Brown, *Tchaikovsky: The Crisis Years 1874-78,* Norton Press, New York, 1983

D. Brown, *Tchaikovsky: The Years of Wandering 1878-85,* Norton Press, New York, 1976

E. Garden, *Tchaikovsky,* Littlefield, Adams & Co., Totowa, 1976

M. Hoffman, *Tchaikovsky* Riverrun Press, New York, 1965

E. Newman (ed), *Modeste Tchaikovsky: Life and Letters of Peter Ilich Tchaikovsky,* Haskell House, New York, 1982

B. Richardson, *Tchaikovsky's Fantasy Overture, Romeo and Juliet,* Grafton Books, London, 1985

W. Strutte, *Tchaikovsky: His Life and Times,* Hippocrene Books, New York, 1979

V. Volhoff, *Tchaikovsky: A Self Portrait,* Taplinger Publishing Co., New York, 1975

J. Warrack, *Tchaikovsky Ballet Music,* University of Washington Press, Seattle, 1980

J. Warrack, *Tchaikovsky Symphonies and Concertos,* BBC Music Guides, London, 1974

H. Weinstock, *Tchaikovsky,* Da Capo Press, New York, 1980

R. Wiley, *Tchaikovsky's Ballets: Swan Lake, The Sleeping Beauty, The Nutcracker,* Oxford Univerity Press, Oxford, 1985

Listener's guide

This section examines in detail some of Tchaikovsky's greatest and best-known works: the music for the ballets Swan Lake, The Sleeping Beauty and The Nutcracker, the 1812 Overture and the 'Pathétique' Symphony. Together with sections on great interpreters of Tchaikovsky's music and specific aspects of musical development of relevance to the works under discussion (for example, the use of unusual musical instruments and the development of the concerto), the descriptions of the pieces of music can be read independently as an examination of Tchaikovsky's musical achievements. However, for the fullest appreciation of this great composer's music, the programme notes are better read before going to a live performance or while listening to the recorded music. The short accounts of the lives and works of some of Tchaikovsky's contemporaries (see opposite) together with the Bibliography and the recommendations for further listening (within the text), suggest further areas of study should you wish to learn more about Tchaikovsky's life, times and music.

Music for the classical ballet

Of all music written for ballet Tchaikovsky's is perhaps the best loved – ranging from the romantic Swan Lake *and the magic of* The Sleeping Beauty *to the lighthearted fantasy of* The Nutcracker.

Throughout his career Tchaikovsky's instinct for theatrical music was on the whole stronger than for the subtleties of the symphonic form. A visit to Glinka's *A Life for the Tsar* when he was ten years old instilled a fondness for opera and left a lasting impression, and when he began to compose, opera was uppermost in his ambitions.

He had constant difficulty in finding the right dramatic subject, but there are nine operas to his name (one in two versions), and two more unfinished. Half of these were composed before *Swan Lake,* the first of the three ballets by which he is now better remembered: the others being *The Sleeping Beauty* and *The Nutcracker.*

'Good ballet music'

Alone among composers for the Russian Imperial Theatres at that time, Tchaikovsky believed that ballet deserved as much musical imagination as he brought to opera. His operas in any case incorporated music for dancing.

He had little respect for the existing general level of ballet music in the Russian theatres, however brilliant the dancing and he had no respect for the music of Cesare Pugni and Ludwig Minkus, each of whom held the official position of ballet composer to the Imperial Theatres, and both of whom relied entirely on facile tunefulness to decorate the dancing.

So when a fellow-composer, Sergey Taneyev, chided Tchaikovsky for passages in his Fourth Symphony that Taneyev thought had 'the flavour of ballet music', Tchaikovsky took issue with him: 'I simply cannot understand why the term should be associated with something disapproving. There is such a thing as good ballet music'.

Tchaikovsky set out to lift Russian ballet from its position as opera's poor cousin. Both The Nutcracker *and* Sleeping Beauty *were composed with invaluable advice on ballet technique from Marius Petipa (below), ballet master in St Petersburg, who dominated ballet for over 30 years.*

Swan Lake (right) has proved Tchaikovsky's most popular ballet. A reworking of an ancient legend of the search for unattainable love, beauty and perfection, it epitomized the ideal of Romantic ballet.

Victor Kennett/Robert Harding Picture Library

Swan Lake

When the idea of a four-act ballet on the *Swan Lake* subject was put to him in 1875, he told his fellow-composer, Rimsky-Korsakov: 'I accept the work, partly because I need the money, but also because I have long had the wish to try my hand at this kind of music'. The art of ballet was then at the peak of its visual splendour in the Russian Imperial Theatres under the influence of Marius Petipa, the French-

born ballet-master at St Petersburg, and Tchaikovsky no doubt felt he could improve on the consistently inferior musical element.

What he lacked at this time was inside information on the way ballet productions worked in the theatre. Later, for the *The Sleeping Beauty* and *The Nutcracker,* Petipa provided Tchaikovsky with detailed specifications on the length of dances, and the rhythms and the moods they should suggest. But *Swan Lake* was virtually

composed as a four-part tone-poem. It brought a stronger and more organic musical element into ballet, but proved initially disconcerting to both orchestra and dancers.

Tchaikovsky had first concerned himself with the subject of *Swan Lake* when he helped to devise and compose a children's entertainment in the summer of 1871, while staying with his married sister, Alexandra Davidova, and her family at their home in the Ukraine. Although no

Reg Wilson

written music from this has survived, there is evidence to suggest that some of the ideas were used again when he accepted the commission for a four-act ballet on the same theme, which occupied him throughout most of 1875 and was finished in the following April.

The captive Swan-princess, half mortal and half supernatural, is an image widely found in folklore around the world, and in balletic terms she is directly descended from earlier Romantic classics such as *La Sylphide* (1832) and *Giselle* (1841), which involve man's quest for an unattainable ideal.

The story for the ballet was probably the joint work of the theatre director, Vladimir Begichev, the dancer Vassily Geltzer, the ballet-master Wenzel Reisinger, who created the first choreography, and Tchaikovsky himself.

At the première in Moscow's Bolshoi Theatre on 4 March 1877, the scenery and costumes were parcelled out among five different designers. The conductor was Stepan Ryabov, who was described by the composer's brother, Modest, as 'a semi-amateur who had never before been faced with so complicated a score', and the choreography by Reisinger was dismissed by one review as 'skilful academic exercises'.

Yet the first *Swan Lake* was not the flop described in some historical accounts. Nikolay Kashkin, who devised a piano arrangement of the music published at the time of the première, later wrote that the ballet 'achieved a success, though not a particularly brilliant one, and held its place on the stage until the scenery wore out, when it was never renewed'.

This included a second version choreographed in 1880 by Joseph Hansen, while Kashkin also noted: 'Not only the decor became ragged but the musical score suffered more and more until nearly a third of the music for *Swan Lake* was exchanged with music from other ballets, and not necessarily good ones'.

In this mutilated form, the ballet continued in the Moscow repertory until 1883, when it disappeared until after Tchaikovsky's death ten years later. A memorial tribute of Act 2 alone, choreographed by Petipa's assistant, Lev Ivanov, reawakened interest in the ballet, and in 1895 Petipa and Ivanov staged an entirely new version of the full *Swan Lake* at St Petersburg which involved changes in the musical structure, made with Modest Tchaikovsky's agreement.

This became the foundation for the ballet's worldwide success, and Ivanov's choreography for the first Lakeside scene of Act 2, has survived more or less intact the world over.

Concert Suite

About five years after its first performance, Tchaikovsky began to think about ways of preserving some of the best of his *Swan Lake* music. He decided to follow the example of the French composer Delibes, whose ballet *Sylvia* he greatly admired.

Since ballet was considered to be an ephemeral genre, Delibes made suites from his ballets for later performance at orchestral concerts.

So in September 1882 Tchaikovsky wrote to his publisher Jurgenson:

The other day I remembered my Swan Lake *and would very much like to preserve this music from oblivion for it contains some quite decent numbers. So I decided to make a suite from it after the manner of Delibes . . . For this purpose I need the piano arrangement and full score of the ballet . . . I will later show you exactly which numbers are to be copied and in what order.*

The suite was published by Jurgenson in 1900, seven years after Tchaikovsky's death, and it is not known whether the composer was in fact responsible for the final selection of the six numbers.

The following programme notes concentrate on the highlights of the ballet, which is world famous. The continuing appeal of this reworking of an ancient legend has fully justified Tchaikovsky's belief that music for ballet need not be in

In Swan Lake, *Siegfried, the hero, vows eternal love to the beautiful Swan princess, held captive by a magician's spell. In a ballroom scene of colourful dances, including an intense Hungarian Czardas (below), the evil wizard tricks Siegfried into breaking his promise. Broken-hearted he rushes to the lake to beg the Princess's forgiveness (right).*

Only a vow of eternal love can break the spell of the evil magician Rothbart, who then appears in the guise of an owl and threatens Siegfried. Siegfried swears his love for Odette and invites her to the ball at the palace. A linked series of six 'dances of the swans' follows including the 'dance of the little swans' and a *'pas de deux, andante non troppo'* for Odette and Siegfried. As day breaks the maidens return to their swan form.

Act 3: Guests assemble in the palace ball-room. The prospective brides are presented to the Prince, who dances with each in turn but refuses to choose one to marry. The magician Rothbart then appears with his daughter Odile, disguised as the Princess Odette. Siegfried, who is deceived by the similarity, is overjoyed, and dances a *pas de deux* with her. This is followed by, or in some versions of the ballet preceded by, a series of national character dances, including a Hungarian *Czardas,* which are probably meant to represent the countries of the prospective brides. Siegfried announces that he has chosen Odile as his bride, unwittingly breaking his vow to Odette. Rothbart turns into an owl and shows him a vision of the true Odette, still bewitched.

Act 4: Odette returns to the swans at the Lake and tells them that she has been tricked. No hope of breaking the spell remains. A storm breaks and a distraught Siegfried finds her and begs forgiveness. There are a variety of endings to the ballet. In one version she dies in Siegfried's arms. In another he fights Rothbart and breaks the spell. In a third Siegfried and Odette throw themselves into the water and are united forever beneath the waves.

any way inferior to music for opera, or less moving than symphonic music. In fact, Tchaikovsky's three great ballets made Russian ballet pre-eminent in Europe.

Tchaikovsky worked on the manuscript for Swan Lake (below) for over a year and it is thought that he included some earlier pieces, written for a children's entertainment.

Programme notes

Act 1: Prince Siegfried celebrates his birthday in the palace gardens. The guests dance a Waltz and then the Prince's mother appears, reproaching him for his levity and reminding him of his duty to choose a wife the following day. The Prince protests but his mother is adamant. After she leaves the party resumes but the prince is downcast. The guests leave and a flight of swans appear to this theme:

Example 1

The Prince and his companions decide to hunt the swans that night.

Act 2: Siegfried dismisses his companions and watches for the swans alone by the lake. As they glide past he is amazed to see them suddenly transformed into beautiful maidens. Their leader, Princess Odette, explains that they have been bewitched into swans, resuming human form at night.

Fotomas Index

Sleeping Beauty

In 1888 Vsevolozhsky, the Director of the Imperial Theatres, suggested *The Sleeping Beauty* as a subject for a ballet to Tchaikovsky. A man of great artistic discernment, he wrote the outline based on the fairytale by Charles Perrault and designed the costumes for it himself. He also brought in the choreographer Petipa who specified each episode in extremely precise detail together with the type of music needed for it.

It seems that these suggestions were a great help to Tchaikovsky, so polished is the final work. And to Mme von Meck, who supported him for many years, he wrote: 'I think, dear friend, that the music for this ballet will be one of my best works. The subject is so poetic, so well suited to musical treatment that I was quite carried away while composing it.'

However, the wider success of *The Sleeping Beauty* did not begin until the lavish production by Diaghilev and his *Ballets Russes* in London in 1921.

Concert Suite

It was just a month after the première of *The Sleeping Beauty* that Tchaikovsky began to think of using some of the music for concert performances. In February 1890 he wrote to his publisher Jurgenson: 'In view of the fact that everyone likes the music of *The Sleeping Beauty* what do you think of the idea of making one or even two suites out of it?'

He suggested leaving the selection of number to the pianist Siloti who had already arranged the ballet for solo piano. In a further letter to Jurgenson, he went on to explain: 'He has great sympathy for my work but at the same time is not

The Sleeping Beauty *tells of the Princess Aurora, cursed at her christening by the evil Carabosse to prick her finger one day on a spindle and die. Thanks to the timely intervention of the Lilac Fairy (below), she doesn't die, but sleeps for a hundred years. Woken by a prince, who has battled through the Enchanted Forest to reach her (illustrated by Doré, above), they marry at a ceremony attended by nursery rhyme characters like Puss in Boots (below right, a costume design), and all the other forest creatures.*

Sotheby Parke Bernet & Co.

the composer, and, composers are almost always mistaken in assessing the value of their works.'

Nothing, in fact was done until 1899, six years after Tchaikovsky's death, when Jurgenson approached Siloti who then arranged a concert suite from extracts of the ballet. The suite, which was designed purely to be listened to, does not follow the sequence of the ballet. The synopsis below, however, outlines the unfolding of the ballet's action.

Programme notes

An orchestral introduction opens with two themes, the first angry and assertive, associated with the wicked fairy, Carabosse (Example 2) and a second, graceful and calm, with the Lilac Fairy.

Guests assemble for the Christening of the Princess Aurora and the fairies each bestow their special gifts. Carabosse enters, furious at not being invited, and proclaims that one day Aurora will prick her finger on a spindle and die. The Lilac Fairy, heralded by the theme from the introduction (Example 3), promises that Aurora will not die but fall into a deep sleep, until woken with a kiss by one determined enough to find her.

Preparations are being made for the Princess's 20th birthday. Despite the fact that spindles have been banned, three

women are discovered with them. The King and Queen enter with four princes, Aurora's suitors. The King condemns the women to death but forgives them when the Queen intercedes. Delighted, the peasants dance a youthful waltz.

Aurora then enters and dances the celebrated *pas d'action,* a ballet scene of a dramatic nature. As she dances for the princes a veiled figure comes forward carrying a spindle. It is Carabosse in disguise. Never having seen a spindle before, Aurora accepts and pricks her finger before her parents can prevent her. The Lilac Fairy appears in the Finale and casts a spell covering the castle with thick forests.

A century later Prince Désiré is hunting in the same forest. The Lilac Fairy appears and shows him a vision of Aurora. The Prince is enchanted and begs the Lilac Fairy to take him to her. They set off together to the gently throbbing Panorama music. He finds the sleeping Aurora and kisses her awake.

Characters from Perrault's other fairy tales come to the wedding of Aurora and Désiré and dance their special character dances. Puss in Boots and the White Cat have a duet, the music suggesting mewing and spitting. The ballet ends with the Lilac Fairy bestowing a final blessing.

The entrance of Carabosse, the wicked fairy (above). In anger at not being invited to the Princess's christening, she places her curse. Twenty years later she reappears at the Princess's birthday party – to offer her the fateful spindle.

The cast of the first production at St Petersburg's Maryinsky Theatre in 1890 (below), featuring Carlotta Brianza (centre) as Aurora. The Tsar came to the preview, and Tchaikovsky later noted the monarch's only comment: 'Very nice'.

Understanding music: composing for ballet

Bringing sight and sound, dance and music, into active co-operation is a complex matter. The more so when the dance form involved is ballet, with its specialized and subtle technique. There are no scores more successful in supporting the full range of ballet than those by Tchaikovsky. Loving ballet and dance, his talent found fresh inspiration in setting music to a specific programme. When composing *The Sleeping Beauty* and *The Nutcracker* he had the stimulus of working to the detailed scenario and notes prepared for him by the choreographer Marius Petipa; they include such requirements as these for the Princess Aurora pricking her finger in *The Sleeping Beauty*:

'When the 3/4 tempo begins (gay and very flowing), Aurora seizes the spindle, which she waves like a sceptre. She expresses her delight to everyone – 24 bars valse. But suddenly (pause – the pain – blood flows!) Eight bars, tempo 4/4 broadly. Full of terror, now it is not a dance, it is a frenzy, as if she has been bitten by a tarantula. She turns and falls senseless. This will require from 24–32 bars.'

The romance and verve with which Tchaikovsky infused classical dancing makes his scores unsurpassed to this day: in terms not only of music but also of theatre they are masterpieces.

Tchaikovsky was writing at the tail end of a long tradition of music composed for the specific needs of theatrical dancing. A giant himself, he stood upon the shoulders of Lully, Rameau, Gluck and Delibes, who had each over the centuries developed the resources of music as accompaniment for dance and for drama. However, early in the 20th century, the great modern dancer Isadora Duncan began to dance to major works of classical music not composed for dance – such as Chopin's piano pieces or Beethoven's Seventh Symphony. By doing so, she changed the course of dance accompaniment, and of musicality in dancing, for the 20th century.

Stravinsky

To this day most ballets are made to existing works of music. It is rare for a composer to write a commissioned ballet score. There have been exceptions, of course. The great impresario Serge Diaghilev (1872–1929) commissioned scores from Maurice Ravel, Igor Stravinsky, Richard Strauss, Eric Satie, Manuel de Falla, François Poulenc, and Serge Prokoviev (among others) during the 20 years (1909–29) in which he presented the *Ballets*

Mauro Pucciarelli

Title page to Delibes's ballet Sylvia, *which Tchaikovsky greatly admired.*

Russes in Europe. Stravinsky (1882–1971) was the most important of these. His first ballet was *The Firebird* (1910) for which he collaborated with the choreographer Mikhail Fokine in exceptional intimacy – according to Fokine, they worked in the same room side by side.

When in 1928 Diaghilev's last choreographer, George Balanchine (1904–83), began to work on Stravinsky's *Apollo,* it initiated the most important choreographer/composer collaboration of the century. This lasted over 30 years, producing such ballets as *Jeu de Cartes, Danses Concertantes, Orpheus* and *Agon.* Stravinsky and Balanchine shared a desire to centre ballet on dancing rather than storytelling, to infuse it with a new power and complexity of rhythm, and to combine frank, fleet athleticism with sparseness of texture – on the other hand, Prokofiev was working in the Soviet Union to keep up the narrative genre of dramatic ballet. Both his full-length works, *Romeo and Juliet* (1938) and *Cinderella* (1945), have since become popular in the West.

But Stravinsky and Prokofiev were not part of any flourishing line of composers working with choreographers. Few compositions today show a subtle responsiveness to dance values, though many works written for dance show remarkable musicality. Although music and dance in the 20th century co-exist, they rarely collaborate with the intensity demonstrated in the ballets of Tchaikovsky and Stravinsky.

The Nutcracker

At St Petersburg, the first audiences for *The Sleeping Beauty* were so appreciative that it was performed on 21 of the 45 ballet nights at the Maryinsky Theatre in its first season. Anxious to follow this success, Vsevolozhsky next invited Tchaikovsky to compose for a double bill consisting of a one-act opera and a two-act ballet. The opera became *Yolanta;* the ballet was *The Nutcracker.* It was based on one of the tales of Hoffmann, the same Ernst Theodor Amadeus Hoffmann who furnished the story for the ballet of *Coppélia,* and who himself

Tchaikovsky based **The Nutcracker** *on one of Offenbach's* **Tales of Hoffman** *and became enthusiastic as he worked on it, composing a concert suite of the music to be released before the ballet. The magical story of the young girl Clara's Christmas Eve dream, in which her Nutcracker doll becomes a Prince and whisks her away to the Kingdom of the Sweets, inspired many designers, such as the renowned Alexandre Benois, to create fantastically ornate sets (below).*

became the central figure of Offenbach's opera, *The Tales of Hoffman*.

Hoffmann's story of 'The Nutcracker and the Mouse King' had been freely adapted into French by Alexandre Dumas the elder as 'L'Histoire d'un casse-noisette', and it was from this version that Vsevolozhsky and Petipa mapped out a ballet scenario, the latter with detailed specifications as in the case of *The Sleeping Beauty*. At first, Tchaikovsky was not attracted to the subject, but he became more reconciled to it as he progressed. Eventually he decided that the music was better than that for his opera 'Yolanta'.

Interest in the ballet was aroused by the concert suite that the composer himself arranged from it and which was performed some nine months before the stage production. Why this happened remains a mystery, unless Tchaikovsky was afraid other composers might find out about his 'secret instrument' which he had specially brought from Paris: the tinkling celesta, its bell-like sound forever to be associated with the Sugar Plum Fairy.

Almost every number in the suite was

Reg Wilson

Once arrived in the Kingdom of the Sweets and welcomed by the Sugar Plum Fairy, Clara is feted by exotic dancers, each representing a different delicacy: the Spanish for chocolate, the Chinese for tea, and the mysterious Arabians for coffee (above).

encored as soon as it was heard, and this 'Nutcracker Suite' later became so popular that the ballet is still sometimes thought to be a confection arranged only to this music, whereas, in fact, the suite contains less than a quarter of the full score.

The full ballet was unknown in the West until a production at Sadler's Wells Theatre, London, on 30 January, 1934, with Alicia Markova and Stanley Judson (followed in 1937 by Margot Fonteyn and Robert Helpmann). Since 1944 it has become a universal favourite, especially at Christmas time, when its dreamlike atmosphere and its evocation of far away, exotic lands rich in sweet and unusual foods, has proved to have lasting appeal.

Programme notes

It is Christmas Eve at the home of two children, Clara and Fritz. *A Miniature Overture* conjures up the world of toys by the absence of all low register instruments. As the parents prepare the tree the children burst in with their friends and there is a lively *March* around the room. An eccentric gentleman arrives, Councillor Drosselmeyer, bringing lifesize clockwork dolls which dance for the children. Clara is given a special present of a doll shaped like a nutcracker. That evening, after the guests have gone, Clara steals down from bed to find her Nutcracker doll. A horde of mice appear led by the Mouse King. The

continued on page 48

Sotheby Parke Bernet & Co.

Since Tchaikovsky's day successive choreographers have embellished The Nutcracker's *simple story-line with new incidents and characters. In Ronald Hynd's 1976 production, performed by the London Festival Ballet, Clara has an older sister and the fantasy is dreamed by both girls (left). Brother Fritz appears in the dream as the commander of a ship (below) that crosses the Sea of Lemonade to the Kindom of Sweets.*

As a ballet about magic, The Nutcracker calls for designs to match its musical and choreographic sparkle. The costume designed by Alexandre Benois for the Nutcracker himself (left) is particularly famous.

In Act II of Ronald Hynd's memorable Nutcracker the Old Woman in a Shoe appears and is presented with flowers (right), while an abandoned bouquet of flowers gives rise to a Waltz of the Flowers (below right). Clara (Anya Gilbert) is in the centre being lifted up by cavaliers.

Nutcracker assembles a force of toy soldiers to fight the mice and a battle ensues. Clara saves the Nutcracker by hitting the Mouse King with her slipper and the Nutcracker is transformed into a handsome Prince who takes Clara on a journey to the Kingdom of the Sweets.

There they are welcomed by the Sugar Plum Fairy. Her short, magical dance to the tinkling celesta is one of the best known in the ballet. Clara's reward for saving the Prince's life is a sumptuous banquet and a wonderfully colourful entertainment consisting of the character dances which make up most of the Concert Suite. These include *Coffee,* an Arabian dance ('cloying and bewitching music', as Petipa specified); a *Trepak,* a lively, Russian dance of Cossack origin; *Tea,* a Chinese dance (an *Allegretto* of the Chinese type, with 'little bells' providing an oriental flavour); a *Dance of the Mirlitons,* a light pastoral dance using little toy pipes; and also a *Dance of 32 Buffoons.*

The *Waltz of the Flowers,* a dance for the Sugar Plum Fairy's attendants, is followed by a dance for the Sugar Plum Fairy and the handsome Prince. The entire company join in the final dances to bring the fantasy to a lively and brilliant conclusion.

There are various endings to the ballet but most frequently Clara is shown asleep by the Christmas tree, clutching her Nutcracker doll, her dream over.

Tchaikovsky's magical Nutcracker *ballet is an enduring Christmas favourite (right).*

Bridgeman Art Library

Great interpreters

Ernest Ansermet and L'Orchestre de la Suisse Romande

Ansermet had one of the most forceful and dedicated personalities of all 20th-century conductors. Born in Switzerland in 1883, it was not until he was in his early twenties that he developed a keen interest in pursuing a musical career. He took his first formal lessons from the composer Ernest Bloch.

In 1910 he gave his first concerts, all in Switzerland, and he began to receive conducting invitations within his own country. By 1915 he had become the conductor of the Geneva Symphonic.

Ansermet was intensely interested in the latest developments in music and quickly established friendships with composers such as Debussy, Ravel and Stravinsky. It was this last composer who recommended Ansermet for the post which would bring him international fame. The conductor was offered, and accepted, the post of Principal of Diaghilev's revolutionary *Ballets Russes.*

During the next three years, Ansermet toured the world with the ballet. His flair and precision had already won him high acclaim. On his withdrawal from the troupe in 1918 he formed his own orchestra — L'Orchestre de la Suisse Romande. Thus began an extraordinary relationship between orchestra and mentor — which continued until Ansermet's retirement in 1966. Within a short space of time Ansermet had drilled his orchestra to the highest standards and these were rigorously maintained.

Ansermet's intensity of vision and intellectual commitment give a unique stamp of authority to his performances, especially the ones where he is directing his own orchestra. His daring and his imagination keep his recorded legacy truly alive and vital for each generation of new listeners.

FURTHER LISTENING

Tchaikovsky Orchestral and Vocal Music

Sextet ('Souvenir de Florence'), op. 70
Tchaikovsky's writing for chamber groups is not generally well-known — his greater successes lay elsewhere. This late sextet, however, is an exception; it was begun during a visit to Italy and subsequently subtitled *Souvenir de Florence.* Sextets are notoriously difficult to write well, and Tchaikovsky was justifiably proud of his achievement. As with all his best work, it is bursting with sweet melodies.

Eugene Onegin (1879)
It is perhaps no coincidence that Tchaikovsky wrote his two most successful operas to texts adapted from stories by Pushkin. *Eugene Onegin* stands out in particular as his operatic masterpiece: no doubt the composer was strongly attracted to the idea of fate which dominates the two central characters, Onegin and Tatyana. With music of extreme beauty and tragic irony their deepest feelings are revealed. The aria in the 'Letter Scene' is one of opera's supreme moments.

Short orchestral works

Tchaikovsky's short orchestral pieces are understandably popular. Here, free from the constraints of larger-scale works, he could indulge his talent as a painter of pictures.

'1812' Overture, op. 49

The idea for the *Festival Overture: The Year 1812* came from Nikolay Rubinstein, the founder of the Russian Musical Society in Moscow. Tchaikovsky composed it in Kamenka in 1880, and it was first performed as part of the celebrations for the Moscow Exhibition of Industrial Arts in 1882. This great exhibition coincided with the consecration of the Cathedral of Christ the Redeemer, built in homage to the Russian victory over Napoleon at Borodino in 1812. Accordingly, Tchaikovsky composed a jingoistic piece, representing the opposing sides in the bloody conflict. However, he claimed to have a low opinion of the work: 'The overture will be loud and noisy, but I've written it without affection or enthusiasm, and therefore there will probably be no artistic merit in it.'

Loud in parts it certainly is, and no one would describe it as an example of great art. It has also come in for more than its fair share of negative criticism, due mainly to the fact that as a popular concert potboiler it has retained its position in the orchestral repertoire for about 100 years. However, with the resurgence of interest in Tchaikovsky's life and music, coupled with the wide range of his works now available on record, someone interested in Tchaikovsky would have to have very selective ears to reach the conclusion that *all* the composer had to offer was music of technicolour, tub-thumping patriotism. Above all else Tchaikovsky was a professional composer with a very sound technique, who worked to commission as well as responding to his inner voice, and who knew how to bring a concept or a programme — here the Russian victory over the French — vividly to life. Most composers have had to work in this way; not all have had Tchaikovsky's success.

In 1880, Tchaikovsky (above) was commissioned to write a work commemorating Russia's victory over Napoleon at Borodino in 1812 (left). He responded with gusto, bringing the subject to life with sounds of cannon and snatches of the Russian National Anthem.

Tchaikovsky composed his sunny **Italian Capriccio** *while on holiday in Rome (above), creating a brightly coloured patchwork of Italian street songs.*

Programme notes

The Overture opens with the hymn *God preserve thy people,* marked *Largo* (very slow) and darkly scored for strings, as Russia prays for deliverance. Then plaintive tags of falling melody on solo oboe are answered by grimly assertive rising phrases from cellos and double basses, as this musical representation of courage in the face of enormous odds grows in strength. A decisive, downward plunging phrase on lower strings and bassoon announces the call to arms. The pace changes to *Andante* (still fairly slow) and over an insistent rhythm on side drum

we hear the fanfares of war, combining later with a broad, confident melody in the upper strings.

The tempo speeds up still further to a vigorous *Allegro* as the main part of the Overture gets underway. It is made up of three smaller sections, all of which are heard twice. The first begins with an athletic passage for strings that is soon reinforced by quotations from the *Marseillaise* on horns,

Example 1

cutting triumphantly through the orchestral texture. This dramatic demonstration of Bonaparte's superior strength is in marked contrast to the next two passages:

the first is a melody that Tchaikovsky had used in an early opera called *The Voyevoda* (1868), the second a dance-like folktune from Novgorod that Rimsky-Korsakov also used in his *Overture on Russian Themes.* Both these melodies could be said to evoke the pastoral serenity of Mother Russia, a serenity now in terrible danger at the hands of the French tyrant.

At its repeat, the *Marseillaise* material has grown in strength, and the two Russian melodies are shorter and sound less stable. The *Marseillaise* begins to dominate – the Battle of Borodino is well advanced – and rises to a climactic statement, with the first soundings of the Overture's celebrated cannon part. A massive unison *rallentando* (a gradual slowing down of pace) on full orchestra leads into the first statement of the Russian National Anthem, together with the victory peals of Moscow's bells:

was merely practising the art of composition.

It was under these circumstances that he left for Rome early in 1880, where he quickly fell to work on the *Italian Capriccio*. The inspiration and model for this work is the second of the *Spanish Overtures* by Mikhail Glinka (1804–57), the founding father of the 19th-century Russian nationalist school of composing. Accordingly, he uses folk melodies and street songs, adapted to fit a colourful collection of vividly orchestrated sections, skilfully linked together to form a whole.

Programme notes

The *Capriccio* opens with a bright, strident fanfare marked *Andante un poco rubato* (slow, in not too strict a tempo), followed by triplet wind chords that form the accompaniment for the first part's passionate and evocative main melody.

This section closes with a return to the fanfare, and a muted recall on cor anglais and bassoon of the main tune leads into the second part (*pochissimo più mosso* – very slightly faster). Over a simple 'oompah' accompaniment, the oboes strike up with a cheeky little tune that, Bolero-like, gathers weight as the rhythm becomes more catchy and the accompaniment busier. This part closes with huge triplet chords, dramatically

pounded out on full orchestra, which subside to a more springy rhythm on the strings alone, announcing the third section, an *Allegro moderato*. Tchaikovsky is gradually accelerating the tempo to suit the verve and dash of the Neapolitan song that follows the incisive melody first heard on the flutes.

A return to the passionate melody from the opening of the work, marked *Andante* with a triplet accompaniment, is a brief respite before the music gathers itself together for the fourth and final section, a whirling tarantella, a lively dance in perpetual motion. One brief, rather strange, interlude for oboes over a droning bass, like a street hurdy-gurdy, momentarily breaks the flow. But soon the tarantella is rushing headlong to a reprise, marked *Allegro moderato* (fast but steady) of the cheeky oboe tune from the second part, now transformed to sound like a stately processional dance. The tarantella returns *presto* (very fast), accelerating to the breathless, exciting *prestissimo* with which the work ends.

Tchaikovsky wrote to Madame von Meck from Rome: 'I think I can predict a good future for it (i.e. the *Italian Capriccio*). It will be effective thanks to the delightful themes which I managed to get hold of, partly from collections and partly from what I'd heard myself on the streets.' He knew how to show melody to its best advantage, and the combination of the *Italian Capriccio's* effortless lyric flow with sparkling, witty orchestration has indeed guaranteed 'a good future for it'.

The sparkling final section of the Italian Capriccio **bursts into a lively and breathless Italian dance (below).**

Russia is saved! The ensuing *Allegro vivace* transforms the earlier fanfare for the call to arms into an invigorating gallop, and the enemy is put to rout with cannons and the Russian National Anthem ringing double-fortissimo in their ears.

Italian Capriccio, op. 45

Two years earlier, in 1880, Tchaikovsky had composed his *Italian Capriccio,* one of his most sunny scores. He was still in the throes of the disastrous consequences following his marriage in 1877 to Antonina Milyukova, and, apart from the Violin Concerto, much of the music written at this time reflects the numbness he felt as a result of this profound personal crisis. Works like the Piano Sonata and the opera *The Maid of Orleans* reveal an objectiveness and lack of involvement, as though he

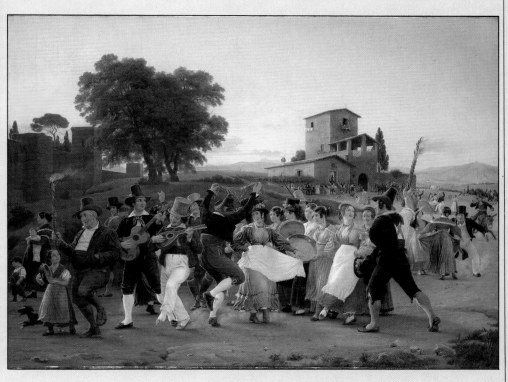

Francesca da Rimini (Fantasy after Dante), op. 32

Tchaikovsky had originally planned to write an opera on Francesca da Rimini, and had got as far as considering a libretto for the project. This was late in 1875 when he was in the middle of working on the ballet *Swan Lake,* which would have prevented him from embarking on the project straight away. Furthermore, on a visit to Paris in 1876 he saw Bizet's opera *Carmen.* Tchaikovsky was greatly impressed by its convincing and modern realism, and resolved to find a story that was similarly realistic, settling a year later for Pushkin's story *Eugene Onegin.*

But Tchaikovsky's interest in the idea of an opera was killed mainly through the insistence of the librettist, the music critic Konstantin Zvantsyev, that the opera should be written in the style of Wagner, to whose music Tchaikovsky showed open antipathy. However, the subject had seized his interest and his brother Modest urged him on during the summer of 1876 to consider the possibility of Francesca as a symphonic poem with a programme.

That summer was particularly depressing for the composer. He went to Vichy for a cure, which he left early, then on to the south of France for a short holiday, and finally to Bayreuth, to review the first complete performance of Wagner's *The Ring.* It was on his way to Bayreuth that Tchaikovsky re-read the fifth Canto of Dante's *Inferno* and wrote to Modest that he was 'inflamed with a desire to write a symphonic poem on Francesca'. After nearly three months of travelling – during which he was often miserable, bored and lonely – he returned with the news that he intended to get married. His resolution was inflexible, and the tragic outcome of his disastrous marriage to Antonina Milyukova about a year later unavoidable.

It was under this emotional strain that he set to work on *Francesca da Rimini;* within three weeks, towards the end of October 1876, the work was finished. The

In Francesca da Rimini, Tchaikovsky created one of music's most tender and tragic love themes. He took his inspiration from the scene in Dante's Inferno where Paolo and Francesca (right) sit together reading the story of Lancelot and Guinevere. Francesca, unhappily married to the tyrant Rimini, is still deeply in love with her husband's younger brother, Paolo. As they read of the moment when Lancelot and Guinevere first kiss, the book falls from their hands and they embrace. Seconds later they are both dead, slain by Rimini in a jealous rage.

On his way to Bayreuth to review the first complete performance of Wagner's The Ring, Tchaikovsky had read the story of Francesca da Rimini. Later he was to admit that although he disliked Wagner (below) and had responded with 'marked antipathy' to The Ring, he had written Francesca while very much under its influence.

Having succumbed to earthly passion, Paolo and Francesca enter the realm of eternal darkness. William Blake's illustration of the Vestibule of Hell (left) conjures up the anguish of the condemned souls. They wait, hands clasped in fear and heads bowed in sorrow, to be ferried across the river Acheron that encircles Hell.

complete score was ready in November, and after its first performance in March 1877 its success was assured.

Programme notes

The score is prefaced with 22 lines from the fifth Canto of Dante's *Inferno,* starting with the lines,

Nessun maggior dolore, Che ricordarsi del tempo felice Nella miseria. (There is no greater sorrow than to be mindful of the happy time in misery.)

a sentiment that was especially poignant for Tchaikovsky at this time.

The Canto describes how Dante, entering the second circle of Hell, sees the souls of those who had abandoned themselves in mortal life to sensual passions being punished by raging storms in eternal darkness. Among them are the shades of Francesca da Rimini and her lover Paolo. Forced into marriage with Rimini, a jealous tyrant, Francesca still could not forget her love for her husband's younger brother, the handsome Paolo. One day, as they were reading together the story of Lancelot and Guinevere, and of the moment that Lancelot

kissed his love, the book fell from their hands and Francesca and Paolo embraced for the first time. Rimini suddenly entered the room and killed them both in a passionate fury.

The formal layout of the symphonic poem is straightforward. A slow Introduction opens out into an *Allegro vivo* (fast and lively) of great force that flanks both ends of the lyrical middle section. The Introduction (*Andante lugubre* – slow and gloomy) represents Dante entering the impenetrable gloom of the second circle of Hell. Over a sinister lumbering bass, chords on brass and woodwind sigh pathetically. However much Tchaikovsky had protested his dislike of Wagner's music, this Introduction, with its restless, questing harmonies and orchestral palette, captures very precisely the mood and sound world of *The Ring.*

The slow Introduction yields to slightly faster music (*Più mosso. Moderato* – with more movement. Moderately) as Dante becomes aware of the despairing souls wailing in torment. One of the storms which perpetually buffets those who surrendered themselves to the throes of earthly passion gathers force over long, sustained notes in the bass. There is a momentary lull as a unison descending figure in the lower strings heralds a brief return to the sighing wind chords. Then with a change of time signature and tempo marking (*Allegro vivo* – fast and lively), the storm quickly draws nearer.

Here the style is unmistakably Tchaikovsky's own as he builds up the tension. A dramatic, plunging motto in the bass alternates with mournful wails and sighs from strings and woodwind; the sense of relentless power is increased as the trombones and tuba enter fortissimo with a short, wild and doom-laden theme. Then, *fff,* the storm breaks, full blast, with a fully realized theme that Tchaikovsky has carefully prepared with fragments of melody that have gradually taken shape from the Introduction onwards.

This is some of the most vivid storm music ever written; we can feel the wind as it rushes through the score. Gradually the fury abates, and we hear once again the

Dante and Beatrice, overwhelmed by pity (below), look on as the ghosts of Paolo and Francesca are whirled away by one of the violent storms that perpetually buffets damned lovers. This Gustave Doré illustration (right), which Tchaikovsky had in mind when he composed the storm music, dramatically conveys the tragedy of the scene.

brass and woodwind chords of the Introduction. The tension relaxes further as a short winding melody for solo clarinet announces the opening of the middle section, Francesca's love music (*Andante cantabile non troppo* – with singing tone, not too slow).

This is one of the greatest single spans of melody that Tchaikovsky had hitherto conceived, conveying at the same time and with unerring insight both the melting beauty of Francesca and Paolo's love and the cruel tragedy of their terrible punishment. The clarinet, accompanied by pizzicato strings, has the first phrase of the melody, answered by a passionately soaring phrase on the violins.

Example 3

After a mysterious link passage, the main tune is repeated complete, this time with richer instrumentation. Now the cellos, near the top of their range and with a graceful, filigree accompaniment from the flutes, expand Francesca's love theme, leading to a section with a prominent part for the harp that develops the mysterious link passage. The music adds strength to a further repeat of the love theme, now with full orchestra, a statement of passionate conviction that has all the fire and tragedy of the love music from Tchaikovsky's earlier *Romeo and Juliet.* The music subsides as Francesca ends her sad narration; distant horn calls hint at the return of the storm, and with a dramatic fortissimo outburst the lovers' ghosts are suddenly whirled away. Bleakly ominous chords on the brass, again with a strong Wagnerian flavour, prepare for the storm, the repeat of which rushes the symphonic

poem headlong to its violent, implacable close.

When he had finished *Francesca,* Tchaikovsky wrote to his younger brother Modest, himself homosexual and Pyotr's closest confidant: 'I have written it with love, and the *love* (i.e. the middle section) seems to have come out respectably.'

Besides gaining immediate popularity with its audiences, *Francesca da Rimini* also won Tchaikovsky generally favourable reactions from critics and fellow composers, who praised its success as programme music. The composer César Cui (1835–1918) commented on the influence of Wagner, to which Tchaikovsky replied: 'The observation that I wrote under the influence of *The Ring* is very true. I myself felt this while working on it . . . Isn't it strange that I should have fallen under the influence of a work of art for which I feel, on the whole, a marked antipathy.'

Understanding music: unusual instruments

Although he was certainly not alone in his desire to explore novel sound-effects, it was Mozart's father, Leopold, who composed the first work of such a kind that is generally known: a 'Toy' Symphony (long attributed to Haydn) in which bird-noises, toy trumpet and drum are used to comic effect in conjunction with a normal string orchestra. Mozart undoubtedly inherited a delight in unusual sounds from his father; many of his works include unorthodox novelties, from the enchanting magic bells and Papageno's pan-pipes in *The Magic Flute* to the sleigh bells and post-horn he used in one of his German Dances ('Sleigh Ride'). He also welcomed the invention of completely new sound-resources and wrote pieces for the glass harmonica and the mechanical organ.

Even Beethoven was not immune to the novelty of the unorthodox and the so-called 'Battle' Symphony was originally intended for a vast mechanical instrument, the Panharmonicon, a strange predecessor of the Wurlitzer organs regarded as essential to classy cinemas in the 1930s.

The mid-19th century was an age of technological invention in many fields, not least that of the orchestra. For instance, Wagner persuaded an instrument-maker to produce a whole family of tubas to enrich the brass section. But perhaps the best-known examples of truly unusual orchestral effects during this period are to be found in Tchaikovsky's music, not only in the cannons and muskets he used in the '1812' Festival Overture, but, more musically, in the enchanting dances of the Sugar-Plum Fairy where the celesta and the bass-clarinet make a memorable début in the symphony orchestra.

Not surprisingly, the 20th century has seen substantial additions to the sound resources available to or demanded by composers, and here a line should be drawn between genuinely musical novelty and comic eccentricity. When Schoenberg asks for the clank of chains in his immense score, the *Gurrelieder,* or when Mahler calls for a hammer-blow in his Sixth Symphony, the intention is completely serious and, in the event, dramatically effective. Vacuum-cleaners in Malcolm Arnold's *Grand Grand Overture,* written for a Hoffnung Festival concert, do not fall into the same category, neither do the typewriter and policeman's whistle Satie used in his ballet, *Parade,* nor the klaxons in Gershwin's *An American in Paris.* On the other hand the teacups hung on a string which Benjamin Britten used to simulate raindrops in *Noye's Fludde* come halfway between the comic and the serious: at first we smile at the childish simplicity of the idea, then realize how truly effective it is.

The electronic revolution of the last few decades has transformed music. One of the first electronic instruments to be offered as a potentially serious addition to the orchestral family was the Ondes Martinot, so called after its inventor, Martinot. The sound is produced from a ribbon along which the performer slides a ring; many different types of sound can be created, but the instrument excels in the production of weird, supernatural sound effects. An early forerunner of the synthesizer (which has now become a ready tool in the endless quest for new sounds) it proved a boon to composers of music for horror films. However, it has also been scored for in more serious music. The Swiss composer Arthur Honegger used it in his dramatic oratorio, *Joan of Arc at the Stake,* as did the French composer Olivier Messiaen in his grand 'Turangalîla' Symphony.

The late British cartoonist, Gerard Hoffnung, organized music festivals for which he commissioned composers. An attempt at performing a Vacuum Quartet in A Flat – 'The Hoover' – (right) for two vacuums in F, one in E flat and a contra vacuum in B flat was made by the renowned Amadeus Quartet (not illustrated here) in 1976.

In June 1876 Turkey invaded Serbia, and before long Russia, outraged by reports of Turkish atrocities, was drawn into the bloody conflict. Thousands of Russian volunteers were enlisted and people avidly read the war dispatches (right). Amid this blaze of patriotic fervour, Tchaikovsky wrote his Slavonic March, which opens with a grim funeral march (below).

Slavonic March, op. 31

After his return from Bayreuth and before setting to work on *Francesca da Rimini*, Tchaikovsky had written his Slavonic March, op. 31. Usually rather slow off the mark in his response to political matters, he could not fail to get drawn into the overwhelming sympathy felt by the Russians towards the Serbs, whose country had been invaded by Turkey in June 1876. Reports of Turkish atrocities grew to the extent that it seemed that Russia would be officially drawn into the conflict; as it was, many Russian volunteers were flocking to Serbia's side.

Nikolay Rubinstein, who had been so vigorously critical of Tchaikovsky's First Piano Concerto the previous year, was planning a charity concert mounted by the

Russian Musical Society in Moscow to help fund the volunteers and to ease the sufferings of the wounded, and had approached Tchaikovsky for a new piece for the concert. Fired by patriotic zeal, Tchaikovsky rallied from the despondency of his unhappy summer and within the incredibly short time of five days, during the first week of October, the Slavonic March had been composed and orchestrated.

Programme notes

Like *Francesca da Rimini,* albeit on a smaller scale, the Slavonic March (originally called the Serbo – Russian March) is in ternary form, where a contrasting middle section is preceded and followed by roughly the same material. Naturally enough, Tchaikovsky chose to base his

march on Serbian folktunes, combining them with the National Anthem *God save the Tsar* (which he also used in the '1812' Overture) and other melodic material.

The work opens with a harrowing death march (*Moderato in modo di marcia funebre* – at a moderate pace in the style of a funeral march), whose heavy-limbed melody expresses all the hardships endured by an oppressed people. We hear this melody three times, in various orchestral guises, before a new melody, in the major and with a shimmering, staccato accompaniment in the brass, injects elements of hope and resolution. A link passage follows, demonstrating Tchaikovsky's unrivalled skill in quickly whipping up tension; strings and woodwind toss a scrap of melody around among themselves with increasing speed, while in the middle of the orchestra the brass fanfares become increasingly louder and more menacing.

All this is underpinned by a quiet though insistent dominant bass. The dominant, a perfect fifth above the home note (the tonic) is the note to which a melody is most naturally and acoustically attracted after moving away from its home base. To sound the note for any length of time makes the listener want to hear the music released back to its home key. This is called dominant preparation, and is a simple and effective means of generating suspense and building towards tremendous climaxes.

The climax here is the return to the opening funeral march, this time defiantly fortissimo, punctuated by savage, synco-

pated (off the beat) chords on the brass, but which still has enough left in reserve for a still louder, more terrifying repeat of the tune. This time Tchaikovsky uses full percussion and a brass accompaniment that echoes the fateful rhythm of Beethoven's Fifth Symphony.

The central section starts with a complete change of mood. A cheerful folktune on clarinet is passed around the brass and woodwind, and quickly gathers substance when transferred to full orchestra, as the tuba and strings in unison intone part of the Russian National Anthem. There follows a note-for-note repeat of the earlier link passage marking the close of the middle section and the reprise of the funeral march theme.

After the brighter music in the major, Tchaikovsky introduces a new melody, at the same time changing the tempo marking to *Più mosso. Allegro* (faster, with more movement), and the key signature to B flat major (instead of B flat minor). The new melody, confident and simple, is played by the horn, with a cheerful woodwind accompaniment; it is repeated with reinforcements, when once more we hear the rousing Russian National Anthem, this time played complete. The victorious coda brings the Slavonic March to a rowdy and tumultuous close.

Madame von Meck, Tchaikovsky's patroness and close confidante, was to write about the Slavonic March: 'I cannot describe how happy this exultant music made me; tears sprang to my eyes.'

Great interpreters

Bernard Haitink (conductor) and the Concertgebouw
The Concertgebouw, under the skilful baton of its conductor, Bernard Haitink, bring a full-blooded sensibility to these short works, yet there is never a moment when their expansiveness lapses into bombast – a particular risk with the 1812 Overture. It is typical of Haitink's approach that the underlying lyricism of the music and the many subtleties of its orchestration are both highlighted.

FURTHER LISTENING

Tchaikovsky Incidental Music

Piano Trio in A Minor, op. 50
Early in 1882 Tchaikovsky's friend and counsellor Nikolay Rubinstein died. This loss is mourned in the Piano Trio, the only work for this combination he ever wrote. It is a work of mixed success, and there are some moments where the heaviness in the writing for the piano threatens to bury the violin and cello. But the first movement, the *Pezzo Elegaico,* contains truly graceful and heartfelt melodies which are carried by the strings to a sensitive piano accompaniment. But the real tribute to Rubinstein lies in the *Variations* movement and its constant elaborations on Russian folk material.

'Manfred' Symphony, op. 58
Tchaikovsky had a deep distrust of programme music, and it took some time before the idea of a symphony written to the story of Byron's *Manfred* took a real grip. But once he started, the tale's dark implications inspired him to one of the great programme symphonies of the century. Within the breadth of the four movements, the composer summons up a brooding and resonant picture of the hero, then gives vent to some of his most successful musical portraiture as he follows Manfred's fate. The revels of the Finale perhaps recall Berlioz's *Harold in Italy,* but are nonetheless pure Tchaikovsky in their expressive colouring.

The Lieder
The song was an art form much utilized by Russian composers in the mid to late 19th century – often to great effect. Tchaikovsky's extensive body of songs, though hardly as well-known as his ballets, still merit close attention. His most famous song, *None But The Lonely Heart,* has been performed by all the great lieder singers.

Symphony no. 6 in B minor, op. 74: 'Pathétique'

Tchaikovsky's failure to come to terms with his own nature seems to be the theme of the despairing Symphony 'Pathétique' – a deeply subjective work which can be regarded as his personal requiem.

I awfully want to write some sort of grandiose symphony which would, as it were, crown my creative career. I've long had a vague plan for such a symphony in my head. I hope I shan't die before I've carried out my intention.

Those revealing words, written to the Grand Duke Constantine in 1890, a year or so after the completion of Tchaikovsky's hugely successful Fifth Symphony, are the first indication we have that he was busily formulating ideas for a sixth: 'something concerned with 'LIFE'', he scribbled down a short time later; 'First part – all impulsive passion, confidence, thirst for activity. Must be short. (Finale, DEATH – result of collapse.) Second part, love; third, disappointments; fourth ends dying away (also short).' Such was his fundamental concept anyway, and for two years it haunted him. He even decided upon the key – E minor.

It was not, however, until part way through 1892 that anything at all substantial emerged and by then Tchaikovsky had sunk so far into one of his recurrent depressions that he decided to abandon the score altogther on the grounds that it was 'empty note-spinning, without inspiration'. (The first movement was subsequently cast as the Third Piano Concerto and the whole symphony later re-constructed by Semyon Bogatyrev and published in 1961).

Emotional turmoil

1892 was in general not especially kind to Pyotr Il'yich Tchaikovsky. For one thing he had never completely recovered from the abrupt termination of his extraordinary relationship with Madam Nadezhda von Meck – the mysterious and generous patroness whom he never met. Then there was his persistent hypochondria, to say nothing of the emotional turmoil that periodically threatened to consume him – not least the doubts and guilt he harboured as to his own true sexuality. Frequent trips to Europe did nothing to assuage these and other problems. Indeed they served only to promote acute homesickness.

Far worse than anything, though, was his inability to compose, the fear – as he put it to his favourite nephew, Vladimir 'Bob' Davidov – that his inspiration might finally have run dry. In December of that year, 1892, the universal hostility meted out to his opera *Yolanta* and ballet *The Nutcracker,* on the occasion of their double-première, brought Tchaikovsky that much closer to breaking-point. It confirmed his deepest insecurities at a time when his dwindling confidence was in urgent need of regeneration.

1893 at first showed little sign of improvement. Indeed, in the early part of February, convinced that there was no future for him, he returned to his country house at Klin and wrote despairingly to his brother Modest: 'What I need is to believe in myself again for my faith is shattered and it seems to me that my role is ended'. Suddenly, and quite inexplicably, a dramatic change of heart came over him and exactly one week later he was back at his desk with fresh ideas for a Sixth Symphony, this time in the key of B minor. 'Bob' Davidov was the first to receive the glad tidings:

During my stay in Paris last December I had the idea of writing a programme symphony; but to a programme that should remain an enigma to everyone but myself. Let them try to guess it! For my part, I intend to call it simply 'Programme Symphony'. The theme of it is full of subjective feeling, so much so that as I was composing it mentally during the journey, I frequently wept.

As soon as I arrived I set to work, with such ardour that in four days the first movement was done and the rest was clearly thought out in my head. The first half of the third movement is just finished. There will be numerous innovations from the formal point of view: the finale, for instance, is to be, not a noisy allegro but a long adagio. You cannot imagine what bliss I feel at knowing that my time is not yet up and that I can still work. Of course I may be wrong but I don't think so.

The dark, despairing Symphony 'Pathétique' is a vivid expression of Tchaikovsky's emotional suffering in the year leading up to his death. This portrait (right), dated January/February 1893 – one of the most authentic of the composer – has graphically captured Tchaikovsky's brooding state of mind. Modest immediately recognized in it his brother's 'cold, dark, intense gaze'.

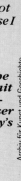

'The most sincere of all my works'

He was, of course, *not* wrong and Symphony no. 6 continued to progress at speed, despite one or two unavoidable interruptions — conducting engagements to fulfill in Moscow and, during May and June, a pre-arranged trip to England where he was to collect an honorary degree from Cambridge University (along with Grieg, Saint-Saëns, Boito and Bruch). However, his usual difficulties with orchestration not withstanding, the completed score was ready by the end of August and Tchaikovsky was able to write triumphantly to his

publisher Jurgenson: 'On my word of honour, never in my life have I been so pleased with myself, so proud, and so happy in the knowledge that I have really created something good.' He then wrote to 'Bob' Davidov, 'I definitely regard [this], as quite the best — certainly the most sincere – of all my works. I love it as I have never loved any one of my musical offsprings before.'

Admittedly Tchaikovsky was wont to make extravagant declarations of this kind before most of his major works only to grow thoroughly dissatisfied with them shortly after their first performances. This time, however, he was right and posterity would come to share his love and admiration for the Sixth Symphony. He was also right, however, in predicting the kind of response that this most unorthodox of symphonies might initially provoke: 'To me it will seem quite natural, and not in the least astonishing, if this new symphony meets with abuse or scant appreciation at first.' Sure enough, at the first performance on 28 October 1893, the public and press alike were lukewarm to say the least. 'It didn't exactly fail to please', wrote Tchaikovsky to his publisher, 'but it aroused some perplexity.'

Indeed it did. For one thing his audience were nonplussed at the presence of a sombre slow movement as a finale. Gustav Mahler and others would nobly make use of such a device in the years to come but at the time, Tchaikovsky's decision to do so represented a bold and courageous break with tradition.

Tchaikovsky's favourite painting (above), which still hangs in his bedroom at Klin, is a telling illustration of his tendency towards self-indulgence.

Novosti

Mélancolie

Tchaikovsky dedicated the 'Pathétique' to his beloved nephew 'Bob' Davidov (right – with the composer), the delight of his last years. Perhaps the happiness that he experienced in Bob's company is expressed in the second movement, which, according to Modest, dwells on the 'fleeting joys' of his brother's life. These lighter moments find a colourful parallel in Redon's Evocation of Butterflies (left).

Novosti

Archiv für Kunst und Geschichte

Novosti

Tchaikovsky, in optimistic mood, sent the score of the Sixth Symphony (left) to his publisher Jurgenson (above). He had decided to call the work 'Pathétique', but then asked for the title to be removed. However, his request was ignored.

Then of course there were the mysterious rumours circulating as to his Symphony's 'hidden meanings'. Tchaikovsky absolutely refused to be drawn on that issue. Indeed, when Rimsky-Korsakov approached him after the performance and asked him outright whether or not he in fact had a programme for his Symphony, he simply replied that 'there was one, of course, but that he did not wish to announce it'. The music, he reiterated, must speak for itself. Only one critic at that first performance was unreserved in his praise of the new symphony; the rest collectively subscribed to the view that, in terms of inspiration, it fell 'far below' its predecessors.

For once in his life, though, Tchaikovsky was not despondent over the notices; he brushed them aside secure in the belief that this Symphony was 'the best thing I have ever composed or ever shall compose'. The morning after the concert, Modest found his brother at the breakfast table in 'excellent spirits' with the score in front of him:

He had agreed to send it to Jurgenson in Moscow that very day, and could not decide upon a title. He did not want to designate it merely by a number and had abandoned the idea of calling it 'a programme symphony'. 'Why programme', he said, 'when I do not intend to give it?' I suggested 'tragic' as an appropriate title. But this did not please him either. I left the room while Pyotr Il'yich was still in a state of indecision. Suddenly the word 'pathétique' occurred to me, and I returned to suggest it. I remember as though it were yesterday how my brother exclaimed: 'Bravo, Modest, splendid! Pathétique!' Then and there in my presence, he added to the score the title by which the Symphony has always been known.

What Modest does not reveal is that within hours Tchaikovsky changed his mind and wrote to Jurgenson asking that the title page should bear a simple dedication to his nephew, the number of the symphony itself and the composer's name – no more. Jurgenson ignored this request and, of course, the title *Pathétique* has prevailed to this day.

Programme notes

To what extent, then, is Tchaikovsky's *Pathétique* Symphony autobiographical? Had the composer knowingly mapped out his own destiny in this music? Did he experience a presentiment of death? Did he commit suicide, as 'some recent evidence has suggested? These and other such questions have been endlessly discussed, supported and contradicted over the years. We shall probably never know the whole truth.

All we do know is that on the morning of 2 November 1893, Tchaikovsky awoke with what appeared to be acute indigestion. At lunch, unable to eat, he insisted upon drinking a glass of unboiled water despite the scare of a cholera epidemic in the city. That night he became very ill and Modest summoned the best doctors in St Petersburg. Within a few days he was dead, and 'Bob' Davidov was one of those at his bedside. 'His sudden death was a blow to one and all', wrote Rimsky-Korsakov. 'Soon after the funeral, the Sixth Symphony was repeated at a memorial concert with Napravnik as conductor. This time the public greeted it rapturously . . .'

1st Movement – Adagio – Allegro non troppo
Tchaikovsky's Sixth Symphony begins as it ends – in darkness. From the lowest depths of the orchestra a murmur of double-basses ushers in the first movement's principal theme: a desolate plaint for solo bassoon which seems to carry with it all the sorrows of the world. From this spare, simple figure the entire movement will germinate. Almost immediately the composer launches an animated, indeed neurotic, discussion of his opening material. The troubled spirit stirs and one senses stress and conflict in the offing. A sudden climax is reached but quickly subsides.

Now the consoling second theme enters – a symbol of love and truth, the good things in life – and arguably the most famous of all Tchaikovsky's melodic creations.

Example 1

At first this lovely melody speaks only of uncertain joy, for the violins and cellos on which it is played are muted *(con sordini)*. Gradually, though, the spirit grows more assertive and 'life', as it were, presses forward in a vigorous clear-headed dialogue for wind instruments (principally flute, clarinet and bassoon) over a pulsing rhythmic motif in the strings.

Confidence restored, the 'love theme' sings out unashamedly now *(senza sordini* – without mutes), its scoring intensified, the effect passionate in the extreme. Its ardour is quickly spent, though, and tenderly a lone clarinet is left to ruminate quietly on the melody once more as Tchaikovsky gently fades the music down to a six-fold *piano* (*pppppp* – as quiet as is humanly possible) on bassoon (usually bass clarinet in modern performances).

Without warning, the entire orchestra virtually explodes into the frenetic development section. Tchaikovsky wrote

Understanding music: naming pieces

It is not really surprising that most listeners prefer to think of Beethoven's Piano Sonata in C sharp minor, op. 27 no. 2, as 'The Moonlight', even though Beethoven himself never sanctioned such a title and was infuriated by it. Correct labels for compositions, giving the opus number and key, lack any imaginative impact, and, more over, accurate labelling can be a problem when scholars make new discoveries. For many years, Dvořák's 'New World' Symphony was habitually known as no. 5 until the unearthing of four earlier unpublished symphonies caused it to be promoted to no. 9. In this case the nickname is justified since the composer himself described the work as 'From the New World', since he wrote it while on a visit to the USA. A clear distinction should be drawn, then, between names endorsed by the composer and those given subsequently. For example, it is perfectly proper to refer to the third and sixth symphonies of Beethoven as the 'Eroica' and the 'Pastoral' because he bestowed these titles himself. However, it is less proper, though admittedly convenient, to call the ninth symphony the 'Choral' because no such word appears on the title-page. Yet 'Symphony no. 9 in D minor, op. 125' seems unnecessarily pedantic for so well-known a masterpiece, and the nicknames given to familiar works stem partly from a mistrust of pedantry and partly from affection.

In the case of Haydn, who wrote more than a hundred symphonies, nicknames do provide a useful means of identification. Even the musically literate might need to pause for thought to identify Haydn's Symphony no. 45 in F sharp minor, but call it the 'Farewell' and even those who do not actually know the music will probably recall that it ends with a gradual depletion of the orchestra until finally there is nobody left.

Some of the names given to Haydn's symphonies may seem surprisingly odd, even funny. The Symphony no. 2 in E flat, the 'Philosopher', was so dubbed to reflect the character of its opening, while no. 82 in C, the 'Bear', takes its name from the theme in the finale suggesting the music of a street performer with a dancing bear, and no. 83 in G minor is called the 'Hen', because the second subject in the first movement seems to resemble a hen's clucking.

Bach's brilliant 'Goldberg Variations' were composed for his pupil Johann Goldberg to play to an insomniac patron. Many relatively humbler personalities have been immortalized thus, especially in the 18th century when musicians were often dependent on affluent and influential patrons. Beethoven's 'Archduke Trio' was written for the Archduke Rudolph, while the three string quartets op. 59 take their name from Count Razumovsky.

Composers in the 19th century were increasingly drawn towards literature or painting as a source of inspiration with the inevitable consequence that descriptive titles became the vogue. Schumann was particularly drawn towards this trend. In 1837, while virtually exiled from his beloved Clara, he wrote a set of dances for the piano, the 'Davidsbündlertänze', each of which was descriptive of an imaginary member of a League of David dedicated to the overthrow of all 'Philistines'. The next year, he wrote the charming and tender pieces of the 'Kinderscenen' or 'Scenes from Childhood'.

In the early part of the 20th century such traditional terms as symphony and sonata fell increasingly out of favour and composers, influenced by the Impressionist school of painting, tended more and more to give their works imaginative titles that would prepare the mind of the listener for the prevailing mood. Debussy, all of whose piano preludes have evocative titles, insisted that they be printed at the *end* of the piece.

The naming of pieces can be taken to absurd lengths, but few have been able to match Satie's eccentric imagination since he published 'Three pieces in the shape of a pear' and 'Dessicated Embryos'.

The freshness of spring inspired Schumann's first ('Spring') symphony.

nothing more desperate, more tormented than this: fear, pain, anguish, determination, all pass before us in a bitter conflict of mounting emotional intensity. The opening bassoon motif has the first word but it is transformed now into a biting *fugato* in the strings (in the style of a *fugue,* with different groups of instruments entering successively with the same fragment of theme). Wildly the music hurtles forward reaching its first peak of hysteria at the point where two trumpets scream out over demented semiquavers in the violins.

There follows a moment's uneasy lull as trumpets and trombones gravely intone a

The third movement is regarded as one of Tchaikovsky's most dazzling creations. It contains some glittering scoring, climaxing in a brilliant blaze of swirling orchestral colour (left).

interlude from the emotional traumas of the first movement. Very quickly, however, it becomes all too apparent that much of the first movement's uncertainty has, in fact, been carried over. Basically, the main body of this movement is cast in the style of a waltz, although the unusual five-in-a-bar (5/4) time signature gives it an appropriately halting, unstable gait.

Nonetheless, the opening themes — initially given out by cellos in their highest register, is a singularly graceful invention depicting, according to Modest Tchaikovsky, the 'fleeting joys' of his brother's life.

Across this 'fleeting' sense of well being, of pleasure, however, the restless middle section, with its throbbing timpani and sighing string melody, passes like an ominous cloud in an otherwise clear sky.

3rd Movement – Allegro molto vivace

In place of a traditional scherzo Tchaikovsky offers — in vivid contrast to the movements on either side of it— one of his most dazzlingly original creations: a scherzo and symphonic march rolled into one. Chattering triplets in the strings launch the mercurial opening passages. All is scurrying, nervous agitation. The textures glint brightly and scraps of the impish march tune can already be heard bandied about the orchestra. A long and skilfully manoeuvred crescendo now ensues, its progress summarily halted though by a smart thwack on the bass drum. At last the march tune takes the stage in its entirety — a jaunty solo clarinet has the privilege — and the main business of the movement gets under way.

Example 3

Gradually gathering strength and impetus in a rising tide of excitement, the march moves inexorably towards its climax decked out in ever more resplendent garbs (rarely does Tchaikovsky command the orchestra with such sheer brilliance). Especially exhilarating are the volleys of rising and falling scales, fired back and forth between woodwind and strings, which usher in the march's penultimate appearance. Then, of

quotation from the Russian Orthodox funeral service (a premonition of his approaching death some believe); but it is offset by anxious shrieks of resistance from the woodwind and whimpering interjections from the strings. Inevitably, the biggest climax of all is soon upon us, its arrival heralded by a frantic eruption of fanfares from the trumpets and horns and a truly heart-rending passage for the strings where each agonizing phrase is passionately answered by the trombones descending lower and lower into their menacing bottom registers.

It is a moment of the blackest despair, yet, as Modest Tchaikovsky put it, the optimist in his brother has not totally deserted him. Very sweetly, very cautiously at first, his romantic second subject (the 'love theme') returns to cast a small ray of hope across the otherwise bleak landscape. The final measures of the movement (the *coda* or tailpiece), a funeral cortège of brass and woodwind over a stalking *pizzicato* (plucked) figure in the strings, are not entirely void of consolation, either. They at least breathe calm, dignity, and some sense of resignation.

2nd Movement – Allegro con grazia

The elegant opening bars would at first seem to suggest a welcome untroubled

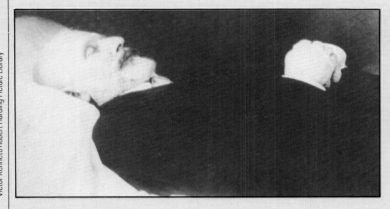

The final movement is a dark song of lamentation, similar, in its chilling intensity, to Böcklin's Isle of the Dead *(right). For many it is associated with death, and in particular the death of Tchaikovsky (left).*

course, there is the thunderous final statement itself and the frenzied closing bars – a blaze of swirling orchestral colour.

4th Movement – Adagio lamentoso

With considerable courage, as we have seen, Tchaikovsky casts his entire last movement as an extended song of lamentation. And how overwhelming it is, following so quickly upon the exuberant display that has just passed. An intense wash of string sound presents us with the opening motif — a descending sigh-like figure which immediately establishes a return to the dark despair of the opening movement. But the pain runs deeper now and the grief is far beyond consolation. Above gently throbbing horns, the principal theme steals in *con lenezza e devozione* (with mildness and devotion) and the emotion rises.

Example 4

violins

pp — *con lenezza e devozione* — *cresc*

mf

A convulsive climax is reached only to be cut off in its tracks by a wild descent of

rushing strings and a decisive blow from the timpani. The intensity re-doubles now as violins and violas reiterate the first five notes of the principal subject (Example 4) and the music slowly yearns its way towards the second and greatest climax. Through wave after wave of sound Tchaikovsky takes his first violins way up into the stratosphere while below them ascending trombones and finally trumpets screw up the tension to an unbearable degree. The final point of release is possessed of a terrible anguish as the composer urgently re-introduces his opening theme against chilling death rattles ('stopped' notes) from the third and fourth horns in their lowest register.

A soft resonance on the tam-tam (large gong) signals the ultimate stroke of fate – or even perhaps the precise moment of death – while trombones and tuba alone mourn the passing. Once more the devotional second theme returns, but this time it wears the home key of B minor, bereft of all hope and utterly grief-stricken. Over and over the composer passes its opening five-note phrase between muted violins, violas and cellos, but the colours are fading fast now and gradually the music sinks back into darkness. One might indeed regard this entire final movement as Tchaikovsky's own personal requiem.

Great interpreters

Evgeni Mravinsky and the Leningrad Philharmonic Orchestra

Born in 1903 and raised in St Petersburg, Mravinsky showed interest in music from the earliest age. By his late teens he was already an accompanist at the Leningrad Ballet School, and at the age of 21 he entered the Leningrad Conservatory to study composition under Scerbachov, and conducting under Gauk and Malko. He remained at the Conservatory as a student until 1930, by which time he had already made his conducting début the previous year. From 1932–38 he was principally associated with the Leningrad Opera and Ballet Theatre, during which time he premiered Shostakovich's Fifth Symphony – the composer's famous 'Soviet artist's

reply to justified criticism'. From that time on he became a champion of Shostakovich's work, and was almost invariably involved in the première of any new orchestral work by the composer.

By the late 30s, Mravinsky was established among the élite of Soviet conductors, winning First Prize in 1938 in the All-Union Conductors' Competition before going on that same year to become Principal Conductor of the Leningrad PO.

After the devastating interruption of World War II to Soviet life, Mravinsky was quick to tour abroad with the Leningrad Philharmonic, reaching the US as early as 1946, and touring extensively through Europe in the mid-50s. He was awarded the Stalin Prize in 1946 in recognition of his service to music in Russia. The Lenin Prize followed in 1961.

Mravinsky has had a long recording career which stretches back to the late 30s. His first record was a complete rendering on 78s of Tchaikovsky's *Pathétique*. Since then, both Mravinsky and the Leningrad PO have recorded a vast array of music.

Mravinsky's approach to his craft is a literal one in that he interprets the music exactly as it is marked in the score, allowing himself no liberties in expression. Thus his performances are often models of orchestral exactness and textural clarity.

With music as dramatic and emotional as Tchaikovsky's, Mravinsky's cool and precise approach is especially effective. While equal to the severest demands of an often turbulent score, he also enables the listener to hear the many normally obscured details of beauty and sensitivity which the score has in such abundance.

FURTHER LISTENING

Tchaikovsky Symphonies

Symphony no. 2, op. 17 ('Little Russian')
Tchaikovsky reached back into the folk-songs of the Ukraine for three of the themes of this symphony; hence its sub-title, the 'Little Russian'. Though one of these is used only in passing, the other two songs are used to help stamp the work with their own particular flavour. The composer, however, avoided writing merely a nationalistic 'folk-symphony', bringing instead his own unique imagination to a work which, despite occasional structural difficulties, has a definite mood and charm.

Symphony no. 4 in F minor, op. 36
This work was written in the aftermath of his near-fatal marriage to Antonina Milyukova, and carries the mental and emotional burdens which scarred Tchaikovsky at this time. It is a programmatic work, based on the idea of the final triumph of the artist over an adverse fate, and shows the composer finally winning for himself a symphonic style which could bear the full weight of expression he felt impelled to give to his music.

Symphony no. 5 in E minor, op. 64
He was a considerably older and more mature man when he wrote his next symphonic work. The Fifth consequently reveals a sense of resignation to his lot and a simple affirmation of faith absent before. This deeply-felt music, full of melancholy, passion and yearning, strives from an emotional equilibrium new to Tchaikovsky. And if the thunderous finale rings a little false in this context, it should not detract from the victories won in the earlier movements.

Longer orchestral works

Tchaikovsky's Piano Concerto no. 1 and the Romeo and Juliet Overture are two of his best-loved compositions. Both demonstrate his passion for melody and give full scope to his expressive powers.

Piano Concerto no. 1 in B flat minor

Grandiose and glitteringly theatrical, the opening flourish to Tchaikovsky's Piano Concerto no. 1 is unforgettable. It is, for many people, the quintessence of Romantic music, along with the equally spectacular opening to Grieg's Piano Concerto. And with the sweeping introductory theme, Tchaikovsky prepares the way for nearly 30 minutes of virtuoso Romantic piano music — in which the heroic pianist struggles alone with grand gestures and seductive melodies to wrest beauty from the instrument.

Tchaikovsky started work on the B flat minor Concerto towards the end of 1874. That year had been relatively quiet. In January, he had completed his String Quartet no. 2, and his opera *Vakula the Smith* had occupied him from June until early September. There was little else. But the completion of the Concerto in December launched Tchaikovsky on a creative stream that was to see four symphonies (nos. 3 to 6), the ballets *Swan Lake, Sleeping Beauty* and *The Nutcracker,* the opera *Eugene Onegin,* the *1812 Overture,* two more piano concertos, a violin concerto and much more.

Yet the B flat minor Concerto was his first venture into concerto form and he was understandably nervous about it. Although he was a capable pianist, he felt unsure about the technical difficulties of the piece. He turned for advice to his friend Nikolay Rubinstein (1835–81) a noted pianist and teacher and also, in a modest way, a composer. It was an unfortunate choice.

In a letter written to his patron Nadezhda von Meck three years later, Tchaikovsky describes how he nervously played through the piano score of his new Concerto to Rubinstein. Rubinstein's reaction was devastating. After sitting in silence throughout the piece, instead of simply commenting on the technical aspects of the music, Rubinstein let fly with a torrent of abuse about the music itself. According to Tchaikovsky, who wrote with the benefit of hindsight:

It appeared that my Concerto was worthless and unplayable; sections were so awkward, so clumsy, so badly written that they were beyond rescue; the work itself was bad, vulgar; in places I had stolen from other composers; only two or three pages could be salvaged; the rest must be thrown away or completely rewritten.

Deeply mortified, Tchaikovsky ran from the room. Rubinstein, realizing he had been too harsh, followed and tried to console him — even offering to play the Concerto if it could be modified. But Tchaikovsky was not to be pacified. He refused to change a single note. And instead of dedicating the piece to

Archiv für Kunst und Geschichte

Society for Cultural Relations with the USSR

Tchaikovsky turned to his friend, Nikolay Rubinstein (above), the great piano virtuoso, for technical advice on his Piano Concerto. Sadly, he was not prepared for the vehemence of Nikolay's criticisms — the pianist pronounced the work 'worthless and unplayable'. Several years later, however, Nikolay admitted that he had been completely wrong, and performed the Concerto in Moscow.

Tchaikovsky (left) soon after he had completed his First Piano Concerto. The work is best remembered for the huge, sweeping tune that launches it – a tune which conjures up the magnificence of Imperial Russia (below).

Rubinstein, as he had originally intended, he addressed it to a young, unknown Russian pianist, Sergei Taneyev. When he had completed the orchestration early in 1875, Tchaikovsky scratched out Taneyev's name and replaced it with that of Hans von Bülow – perhaps because von Bülow, who was a great champion of Tchaikovsky's music, was a more influential figure. And it was von Bülow who conducted the first performance in Boston on 25 October 1875.

The Boston première was a great success and von Bülow immediately cabled Tchaikovsky in Moscow with the good news – a cablegram believed to be the first ever sent between these two great cities. Tchaikovsky immediately sent a reply, but it cost him his last kopeck. Praise was not universal – the leading Boston critic John Dwight asked 'Could we ever learn to love such music?' But the lasting popularity of the piece was assured. Soon it

was being performed all over the world.

Nikolay Rubinstein was gracious enough to admit his mistake and the breach between the two friends was quickly healed. Indeed, Rubinstein conducted the Moscow première. Three years later, on 22 March 1878, Rubinstein actually played the Concerto in a public performance that gave Tchaikovsky a great deal of satisfaction. He had always had Rubinstein's brilliant style in mind when he composed the piece, and the virtuoso did not let him down.

Oddly enough, it has since been discovered that although Tchaikovsky was unwilling to change a single note for Rubinstein, he allowed other pianists such as Edward Dannreuther and Alexander Silote to make quite substantial changes. It seems that the massive sound of the opening theme may, in fact, owe a great deal to Dannreuther's alterations and amendments.

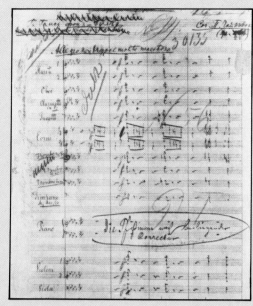

Society for Cultural Relations with the USSR

A page from the manuscript of the First Piano Concerto (above), on which Tchaikovsky began work in November, 1874.

Programme notes

Unkind commentators have described Tchaikovsky's Piano Concerto no. 1 as a 'tadpole' – a great head, and a tail of rapidly diminishing substance. Indeed, there is a 'great head', a mighty opening paragraph of music, in the shadow of which anything would be anticlimactic. Yet the 'tadpole' jibe ignores the considerable skill of the rest of the work, the originality of the first movement, the quiet beauty of the slow movement, the scintillating rhythms of the Rondo. The work may display formal flaws but does not lack substance.

First movement – Allegro non troppo

The opening of the Concerto is indeed impressive. A resounding four-note descent by the brass is repeated three times before the strings sweep into the familiar majestic theme, accompanied by massive piano chords. This theme is played *allegro non troppo e molto maestoso* (not too fast and very majestically). The pianist takes up the melody and embellishes it extravagantly and the music moves forward with almost painful majesty. Then with piano and *pizzicato* (plucked string) interchanges, the original theme is restated to close this opening gesture.

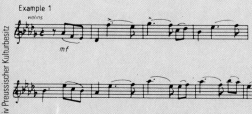

Example 1

Remarkably, this magnificent theme is then dropped altogether and never

Bildarchiv Preussischer Kulturbesitz

After the opening tune dies away, Tchaikovsky introduces a vigorous new theme which recalls the dynamic rhythms of Russian dancing (left). This is thought to be based on a Ukrainian folk-tune, and the fiery Rondo finale also has Ukrainian origins (bottom left). Here, Tchaikovsky has actually quoted from a Ukrainian song: Come, Come Ivanka.

The scurrying central section of the Concerto, based on the old French song 'Il faut s'amuser, danser et rire', was part of the repertoire of Désirée Artôt, the French singer (below) to whom Tchaikovsky was briefly engaged. It is a delightfully frivolous, dance-like section, infused with the same spirit as Lancret's painting (right).

reappears again. Many musicologists have been amazed by this apparent wastefulness – Beethoven or Brahms would never have abandoned such an important theme. It is sometimes suggested that this is a structural error, and that Tchaikovsky really intended to revive the theme later in the piece – even that he added the theme as an afterthought, borrowed from another piece to start the Concerto in grand style. Others have claimed to detect traces of the opening theme in the finale, but none of this really matters – the fact is, this theme provides a glorious curtain raiser to the rest of the Concerto.

As the opening theme dies away, the music pauses amid quietly expectant trumpet calls. An abrupt increase of tempo to *allegro con spirito* (lively and vigorous) announces the first subject, in which piano virtuosity and glittering orchestral writing combine. The theme is thought to be based on a Ukrainian folk tune Tchaikovsky learned from some blind beggars at a fair in Kamenka. Brusque piano chords interspersed with equally brusque strings create a thrilling, dynamic rhythm which is indeed reminiscent of Russian dancing.

A second subject eventually appears on woodwind, at first interrupting but then being taken over by the soloist. But the weight of the rest of the movement is to fall upon yet another theme which, with its dreamy atmosphere and muted strings, recalls the love theme in *Romeo and Juliet.* This leads to an exciting conflict with the orchestra as the development section gets underway. After an extended development, the dreamy melody finally undergoes a sudden and complete change of mood, with a tense interplay between piano and orchestra. Mighty piano octaves gradually diffuse the tension and the soloist muses for a while upon the almost forgotten second subject.

A new idea soon attempts to secure a foothold over a timpani roll, but the third theme returns to usher in a traditional recapitulation in which first and second subjects are recalled. Once again there is a passage of exciting piano and orchestral interplay before the temperature is lowered by the soloist's *cadenza* (a passage which the soloist plays alone to show off his virtuosity). Both second and third melodies are interwoven with new material in this long cadenza, but in the *coda* (closing section) it is the third theme that dominates.

Second movement – Andante semplice

The strenuous activity of the first movement is quelled by the innocence of the second. This is played *Andante semplice,* which means at a moderate pace and in a simple unaffected style, and the strings are muted throughout. It opens with a cool flute melody whose third note is raised from F to B flat as the piano adopts it, and on every subsequent occasion.

Once again, as in the first movement, Tchaikovsky's first idea soon disappears for good, yet the change is at once so subtle and so far-reaching that we cannot help admiring its daring. Here are two entirely

different ways of presenting an idea, achieved by the simple alteration of one short note.

In the middle of the movement stands a lively *prestissimo* (very fast) episode based on the old French song *Il faut s'amuser, danser et rire,* which had been sung by Désirée Artôt, a singer who had attracted the composer's amorous attention some years earlier. It is a scampering, whirling twilit dance – a total contrast to everything else in the Concerto.

Example 2

pp molto cantabile e grazioso

After another sparkling cadenza, the soloist gradually reduces the tempo and moves into a *rubato* passage – where notes are left hanging so long that the listener can hardly wait for the re-introduction of the opening theme to release the tension. When it comes, it receives a lush, romantic treatment, with swelling strings supporting the melody, now played on the piano with elegantly decorative trills. But before it becomes too sugary, an oboe takes over the theme from the piano and its thin, reedy tone adds a touch of piquancy. Then, with distant reminders of the theme from horn, clarinet and flute, the movement finishes on a quiet chord.

Third movement – Allegro con fuoco
The finale is, like so many pieces of Classical and Romantic music, in *rondo form* (a form in which the original theme comes round again many times). It is essentially a dance form and, in Tchaikovsky's Concerto, it is a syncopated Ukrainian dance – or a good copy – that attracts endlessly varied woodwind commentaries upon each repetition.

Tchaikovsky indicated that it is to be played *allegro con fuoco.* 'Fuoco' is the Italian for 'fire' and the piece calls for a fiery, dancing approach.

Early in the movement, the piano introduces the fiery rhythmic tune with staccato chords, soon accompanied by *pizzicato* (plucked) strings. High flute and clarinet runs create a festive air before the whole orchestra takes up the theme with a gloriously robust passage that is to come round twice again in the movement. The tempo then drops slightly and the strings introduce a swirling, romantic melody that provides the second main theme. This eventually forms the basis of a striking *crescendo* (a phrase that builds up to a loud climax) which runs into the pianist's final cadenza before being subjected to the full Romantic embellishment. A brief coda based on the dance tune finds the protagonists, hero and orchestra, in total agreement and jubilant mood.

Romeo and Juliet – Fantasy Overture

With its sensuous love theme and thrilling climax, the *Romeo and Juliet* Fantasy Overture is one of Tchaikovsky's most successful and satisfying compositions. Yet like the Piano Concerto, its creation was beset by criticism.

Just as Tchaikovsky received more advice than he wanted from Rubinstein about the Concerto, so *Romeo and Juliet* was heavily influenced by the criticism of the composer Balakirev. However, Balakirev's role seems to have been a good deal more positive than Rubinstein's. Indeed, it was probably Balakirev who first suggested the idea for the piece.

Inspiration

The two friends had been discussing the possibility of an orchestral work based on Shakespeare's *Romeo and Juliet* during the summer of 1869. But the young composer was going through a creative lull at the time – perhaps he was thinking about Désirée Artôt, the Belgian soprano with whom he had dallied earlier that year.

In October, Balakirev wrote to Tchaikovsky chastising him for his sluggishness. Balakirev even sent him a suggestion for the opening bars of the music – a 'fierce allegro' for the fight between the Montagues and Capulets.

Typically, Balakirev even told Tchaikovsky how to find inspiration for the piece – by arming himself with 'galoshes and walking-stick' and strolling up and down the boulevards of Moscow. Tchaikovsky actually found this little snippet of fatherly advice rather useful and many of his subsequent compositions were thought out while promenading through Moscow. Tchaikovsky got down to work and completed the overture within six weeks.

As for the 'germ of an idea', Balakirev's opening bars, he actually incorporated it in the fight section but so heavily changed that it is barely recognizable. But when he showed the first draft to Balakirev, his adviser was less than flattering. While he was not so abusive as Rubinstein, he criticized many points in poor Tchaikovsky's original conception, suggesting changes here, new phrases there and that some sections should be dropped altogether.

The introduction, Balakirev said, sounded 'like a Haydn quartet', and so lacked the Catholic religiosity that he felt it needed. It would be much better to model it on a Liszt chorale. And the love theme was too blatantly erotic for Balakirev.

Modifications

With Rubinstein, Tchaikovsky had stood firm. But Balakirev was an influential man, head of the Russian school of composers known as 'The Five' and, in the face of his

Popperfoto

It was the composer Balakirev (above) who suggested that Tchaikovsky write an orchestral work based on Shakespeare's* Romeo and Juliet. *He also took an active critical role in the piece's composition.

forcefully proffered advice, together with words of undying friendship and admiration, Tchaikovsky gave way, amending and redrafting countless times. There is now no way of knowing whether his first ideas were sound or not.

Tchaikovsky modified much of the work, but it is not known whether he remodelled the love theme. If he did so, presumably to cool its ardour under the weight of Balakirev's puritanical insistence, the first version must have been sensuous indeed. Either way, Balakirev, like all the world, soon grew to love the theme. In his biography of Tchaikovsky (1973), Edward Garden quotes a letter from Balakirev to Tchaikovsky in December 1869. In the letter, Balakirev says the theme makes him think of 'you wallowing in your bath with Artôt-Padilla herself rubbing your tummy ardently with fragrant soap-suds.'

With all the changes, we might be forgiven for expecting the finished article to sound as if it had been designed by committee, but in the end Tchaikovsky's individual style and genius shine through. And it is generally agreed that Balakirev's advice was often very good. The piece is vintage Tchaikovsky.

Tchaikovsky was often prone to go over the top in places and lapses of taste are common in his earlier works. Although the finale of *Romeo and Juliet* can never be accused of subtlety, it is much more sparing in its instrumentation than some of his works. This is undoubtedly Balakirev's influence at work. The unusual choice of

Ford Madox Brown 'Romeo and Juliet'. Delaware Art Museum, Samuel and Mary R. Bancroft Memorial

The darkly-coloured introduction to the Overture, filled with foreboding, conjures up the image of Friar Laurence (left). He vainly tries to intercede between the lovers' two warring families, in a tremendous orchestral 'swordfight'.

Programme notes

Tchaikovsky's first thoughts may have been close to Shakespeare's original play, but the Fantasy Overture we know today would be suitable as a prelude – if a rather extended one – to an opera on the subject, since various elements are taken from the story to form a coherent symphonic poem, rather in the style of the early-Romantic overture. This descriptive music can not be set to a literary plan; it simply evokes scenes and characters in the play – Romeo, Juliet and Friar Laurence. It does so, however, in a musical plan that, for Tchaikovsky, is surprisingly Classical. The principles of sonata-form are not violated – Balakirev's influence again?

A darkly coloured and rhythmically restrained introduction draws an image of Friar Laurence. The climbing phrases resolve themselves and seem to remain suspended high in the air, as if apprehensive of the ill-starred events that are about to unfold. The Friar's theme moves urgently for a time over *pizzicato* (plucked) strings, but the gloomy atmosphere returns. The music seems destined to proceed to the tragedy. A sudden increase of activity over a drumroll announces the first theme of the Allegro and brings an anxious alternation of string and wind chords. Then the warring families meet to do battle; the music fills with terror – and with masterly scoring.

Tchaikovsky's imaginative scoring may be noticed again at the start of the second subject – the so-called 'love theme' – which is scored initially for the unusual but effective combination of violas and cor anglais. A second part for subdued violins is followed by a fuller statement of the love theme, a yearning horn figure set against flute and oboe in unison. Cor anglais then returns with swelling lower strings and harp as the exposition falls to a close.

In the development section, the sword-fight music is juxtaposed wih Friar Laurence's theme on horns. At the climax, as development gives way to recapitulation, one may imagine the Friar's voice (now on trumpets) raised in anguish over the fighting. At length, the love theme returns, greatly expanded, and comes to a tortured climax, only to be destroyed at its height by the return of the sword-fight music. There is a sudden tragic collapse.

A throbbing funeral march for the dead lovers brings the love theme, now drooping and twisted. There is a funeral oration based upon the second, subdued, part of the love music, and a final reference to the main love theme before fierce jagged chords bring the work to a close.

keys in the love theme is also thanks to Balakirev. But most importantly, Balakirev gave Tchaikovsky the confidence to compose in his own style, and the eight years following the composition of *Romeo and Juliet* were among the most productive in his life.

Not all Balakirev's suggested changes were incorporated immediately and an early version was premièred in Moscow in March 1870 under Rubinstein's direction.

It was an odd première, the day before, Rubinstein had been in court accused of wrongfully dismissing a girl student at the Moscow Conservatory. The girl won her case, and Rubinstein had to pay damages. But his admirers wanted to demonstrate their support for the great musician. They cheered loudly throughout the concert and poor Tchaikovsky's overture went unheard amid the din.

Now it was Tchaikovsky who expressed doubts about the work. With the experience of a concert performance to guide him, he reshaped the piece yet again during the summer months of 1870. A further revision took place ten years later, and this third version, the one familiar today was premièred at Tbilisi on 1 May 1886. The work is dedicated to Balakirev.

The ravishing love theme (left), which crowns the Overture, was considered by Balakirev to be too blatantly erotic. Indeed, its passion and emotional power have made it one of the most famous and expressive themes in romantic music.

Understanding music: what is a concerto?

In the Romantic and Classical eras, the *concerto* was perhaps the most important musical form next to the symphony. Nearly all the major composers but Schubert wrote at least one concerto — Mozart wrote over 30 — and the range of music in this form is enormous.

The most distinctive feature of the concerto is the crucial role played by a single virtuoso instrument. Indeed, some concertos were written as unaccompanied solos, although more usually the solo part is interwoven with a full orchestral score and the soloist seems almost to debate musically with the orchestra.

In the earliest concertos, it was a small group of talented musicians (the *concertino*) and a larger group of mediocre musicians (the *ripieno*) who debated, not soloist and orchestra. But the effect was similar. In the 17th century *concerto grosso* of composers such as Corelli, for instance, the music would alternate between elaborate concertino passages and passages in which the ripieno would join in. The 'all together' sections are called *tutti*.

Virtuoso display

During the Baroque period, however, the concertino was refined to a solo role — although concertos with a concertino appear well into the 18th century, and there has been a revival of interest in the concerto grosso this century. But a solo concerto provided a wonderful opportunity for a virtuoso performer to display his talents — a display with considerable audience appeal. Indeed, many solo concertos in the Classical and Romantic eras were written specifically as showcases for particular virtuosos. Often, this was the composer himself — not surprisingly, since many of the great composers of concertos, such as Mozart, Beethoven and Liszt, were brilliant performers themselves.

The element of virtuoso display is an important feature of the concerto. It is perhaps why, unlike symphonies, concertos rarely include a minuet movement — the structure of the minuet too rigidly restricts the soloist. Indeed many concertos have a *cadenza,* a brilliant passage which the soloist 'improvises' to show off his or her talents to best effect — usually with the orchestra falling completely silent. In the earliest concertos, the cadenza was literally improvised. Mozart and Beethoven would simply provide an outline. Later composers, on the other hand would write out the cadenza in full to avoid the balance of the piece being destroyed by an insensitive soloist — particularly when composing for an instrument they played themselves.

Reg Wilson

Like the symphony, the concerto falls into the sonata tradition (see page 24), but it generally has three movements (fast-slow-fast) rather than four. Some composers, such as Brahms, in his Piano Concerto no. 2, added a fourth, giving the concerto almost symphonic scope. But surprisingly many are in traditional form.

Typically, concertos open with a tutti passage. In many Classical and Romantic concertos, the solo passage that follows simply elaborates on the tutti theme. When the piano enters for the first time in Tchaikovsky's Piano Concerto no. 1, for instance, it simply embellishes the grand opening theme. Some composers, however, notably Mozart, would introduce a completely new theme with the soloist's entry. This immediately sets the soloist apart — a small voice against the might of the orchestra.

In Mozart's concertos, this has a rather poignant effect, but many Romantic composers took up the idea of the lone voice contending with the orchestra to produce a completely different effect. In the Romantic era, the interplay between the soloist and orchestra is more of a struggle than a debate — a struggle that seems to echo the Romantic concept of the hero fighting alone against Fate.

Two developments encouraged, and were encouraged by, this concerto of contention. First of all, the astounding violin playing of Paganini showed the excitement that could be engendered by virtuoso playing. At the same time, the piano developed enormously in power and range, so that by Liszt's day, it could compete with an orchestra for sheer volume — and, of course, Liszt displayed a new virtuoso piano technique as dynamic as Paganini's on the violin.

The excitement of virtuoso violin and piano playing and the power of the piano combined to allow the soloist to struggle manfully against the orchestra. The effect, where it works, is thrilling.

Great interpreters

Sir Colin Davis (conductor)

Sir Colin Davis is one of the most popular conductors today. He is perhaps best known to British audiences through his Promenade concerts. Born in Weybridge in 1927, he studied clarinet at the Royal College of Music and became a bandsman in the Household Cavalry. Although he was barred from conducting classes at the Royal College of Music (because he was unable to play the piano) he persisted in his ambition to become a conductor, taking several odd conducting jobs. In 1957, his persistence was rewarded when he was appointed assistant conductor of the BBC Scottish Orchestra. His Sadler's Wells début in 1958, and two successful concerts at the Edinburgh Festival and the Festival Hall in the following year, effectively made his name.

In 1964, Davis left Sadler's Wells, and from 1967–71 he served as principal conductor of the BBC Symphony Orchestra. In 1971, he succeeded Georg Solti as musical director of the opera company at Covent Garden. He received the CBE in 1965, and was knighted in 1980.

An energetic and intelligent conductor, Colin Davis tends to go for accuracy rather than full-blown romanticism in his interpretation. His best performances are fresh, lively and convincing.

Claudio Arrau (pianist)

Claudio Arrau, the celebrated pianist, now in his 80th year, was born in Chile in 1903. A child prodigy, he studied piano under Martin Krause at Stern's Conservatory from 1912–18. Krause, who was himself a pupil of Liszt's, was to be Arrau's only teacher. The young pianist gave his first recital in Berlin in 1914, and made a concert tour of Europe in 1918. In 1921, Arrau returned to South America to give concerts in Chile and Argentina. He made his London début in 1922, and toured the USA in the following year. In 1924, he himself became a teacher at Stern's Conservatory, remaining on the staff until 1940. A successful USA concert tour in the subsequent year encouraged him to settle permanently in America.

Arrau is recognized as one of the greatest pianists of the last 30 years. He is not a showman, although he has tremendous technique, preferring the deliberate to the spectacular. His performances are always characterized by a great intelligence and depth of feeling.

Boston Symphony Orchestra

The Boston Symphony Orchestra was founded in 1881 by the wealthy Bostonian banker, Henry Lee Higginson. He put one million dollars at the orchestra's disposal, hired Georg Henschel as its conductor and employed 68 fine musicians, who were mainly of German extraction. The first concert took place on 22 October 1881, and was a resounding success.

From these auspicious beginnings, the orchestra has grown to become one of the top three American symphony orchestras, maintaining a consistent standard of excellence. Many distinguished conductors have become associated with it, including Sir Colin Davis who became principal guest conductor in 1975.

FURTHER LISTENING

Tchaikovsky Orchestral Works

Serenade in C for String Orchestra, op. 48

Tchaikovsky's most inspired works always revolved around the statement and development of brilliant melodic ideas, and the Serenade for Strings is a perfect example of this. Freed from the rigorous demands made upon him by the formal designs of the symphony, he allows his love of melody full scope. The result is some 20 minutes of music full of verve and grace, fully utilizing the sweetness and romance inherent in the use of strings alone. Even his severest critics greeted the work with whole-hearted enthusiasm.

Violin Concerto in D, op. 35

After the first Piano Concerto, this stands as Tchaikovsky's most successful and popular piece for soloist and orchestra. Like other great Romantic composers, he thrives on the lyrical rather than the structural in music, and the Violin Concerto is no exception to this rule. Though it is formidable in its virtuosic demands on the soloist, full of testing technical difficulties, it never becomes a mere showpiece, for the instrument is made to emphasize at each turn its individual and basically rhapsodic nature.

Variations on a Rococo Theme for Cello and Orchestra, op. 33

Perhaps surprisingly for such an avowed romantic, Tchaikovsky made no secret of his lifelong passion for the music of Mozart. These Variations, based on Tchaikovsky's own theme written in the 18th-century Classical mode, demonstrate this devotion openly. There are seven variations in all, each one containing finely-balanced thematic interplay between the cello and orchestra. The composer's own individual touch shows in the thoroughly personal way he develops and orchestrates each variation to create a unified whole of great wit, ingenuity and charm.

In the background

Scientists still argue which contributes most to our personalities, talents and behaviour: the inheritance of our genes or the influence of our environment. However, it is undeniable that we cannot help being affected to some extent by our surroundings, both in the narrow sense of our personal backgrounds and in the global sense of the times we live in. Great composers are no exception, and the following pages describe the historical background to Tchaikovsky's life and how political, social and cultural developments influenced and inspired him: the social reforms of Tsar Alexander II, which freed the serfs, and the beginnings of radical and revolutionary unrest in Russia; the major literary achievements of Pushkin, Dostoyevksy and Tolstoy in the flowering of the Russian novel and poetry; the history of ballet, which at this time found its greatest expression and for which Tchaikovsky composed some of his greatest and best-loved music; and the fabulously wealthy high society of the United States whom Tchaikovsky met during his visit near the end of his life.

IN THE BACKGROUND

Life under the Tsars

Until 1861, the majority of Russian people were serfs, tied to the land and literally owned by their landlords. Serfdom was abolished by the reforming Tsar Alexander II, who believed that the institution caused his country to be both socially and economically backward.

Alexander's reforms were opposed by the slavophils who thought that the Tsars, beginning with Peter the Great in the early 18th century, had been wrong to imitate the institutions of western Europe, and that uniquely Russian values were in danger. To some extent this was correct, since the absolute power of the Tsar himself was beginning to be questioned by groups of young radicals. Their agitation and the resulting official reaction led in 1881 to the assassination of Alexander, and the violent attacks on the monarchy continued until the 1917 revolution overthrew the Romanov dynasty for ever.

'Rigorous authority'

In a single decree in 1861, Tsar Alexander II granted freedom to 40 million serfs. Russia had finally accepted the ideal of individual freedom, but had also sown the seeds of revolution.

Defeat at the hands of the French and British armies in the Crimean War (above) meant that Russia was left with no part to play in general European affairs. A humiliated Russia looked for an answer to this national disaster and discovered that society was in need of great social reform

The Crimean War ended in 1856, and defeat left Imperial Russia with an acute crisis of confidence. Her pretensions as a great military power were exposed as sham; her smug belief in the stability of her unique institutions lay in tatters; her plain backwardness in a rapidly changing world was starkly revealed. The chill of despair went wide and deep, and provoked even in the most conservative quarters the realization that things were not as they should be.

It was not that the loss of this particularly inane war left Russia threatened with dismemberment or the yoke of foreign domination. Nothing of the sort. The ramshackle empire stretching from the Arctic to the Caspian, and from the shores of the Baltic to China and beyond to the wastes of Siberia and even across the Bering Straits to Alaska, emerged from the Crimean fiasco pretty well intact. The trouble was that no one who took a serious look at Russian society in the middle of the 19th century could fail to see that this national humiliation was an inevitable consequence of national ineptness. The principal casualty of the Crimean War, in other words, was Russian self-esteem, and in its wake came a clamour for reform.

Russia's internal problem

It was not difficult to identify the failings of Russian society, and indeed many of them were not unique to Russia but only magnified by the sheer scale of the place — a huge and cumbersome bureaucratic machine that was at best irksome and at worst stultifying; an unfair legal system, backed up by secret police, and rife with corruption at every level; an overall economic performance that was pitiful by advanced European standards and steadily deteriorating as the

Industrial Age swung into full stride.

There was, however, one respect in which Russian society was uniquely badly organized. The overwhelming majority of the Tsar's subjects were not free men or women but existed in bondage, either to the land-owning aristocracy or to the state itself. Serfdom – along with black slavery in the United States, the most glaring abuse in the western world – lay at the heart of the Russian malaise. Its harmful effects permeated every aspect of national life, and it was inescapable, therefore, that the drive for reform centred in its abolition.

It is difficult even to begin to grasp the magnitude of the serf problem. At this time the total population of European Russia was 60 million. Of these, nearly 50 million were peasants, and 40 million of the peasants were serfs; that is, they were agricultural labourers who were, to all intents and purposes, the private property of those who owned the land on which they worked.

Russians, even those who detested serfdom, were quick to dispute the parallel between serfdom and slavery, and there were some important differences. But it is surely revealing that the wealth of landowners was commonly expressed in terms of the number of serfs they possessed, rather than in terms of income, capital or acreage. A large landlord would own hundreds of 'souls', and a great one, thousands. The greatest of all, the state itself, owned roughly half the entire serf population, 20 million 'souls'.

Life of the serf

As with slavery, the conditions of life facing a serf varied depending upon the accident of his location and the temperament of his master. He was tied to the land – where he was born he remained. Everywhere, however, certain rules governed his existence.

If he ran away and was caught, and an internal passport system and stiff penalties for harbouring a fugitive pretty well ensured his capture, he would be flogged at his master's pleasure – just as for other offences, real or imagined, since there was no legal recourse for him. Forty lashes with the birch or 15 blows with the stick were stipulated as maximum

Though agriculture was the usual work of the serf, many were hired out to work in mines and factories. Others had to eke out their existence by scavenging for coal (above). They were in bondage to their owners and could be bought and sold like cattle. In the painting The Bargain *(below) a serf is cheaply bought by a noble.*

punishment, but a landlord with a mind to do so could ignore these limits with impunity. Only if he gained a reputation for the most outlandish brutality need he fear any sort of official rebuke. If a landlord considered a particular serf incorrigible, he could have him transported to Siberia or force him into the army, again without legal restraint.

The serf's working life was split between farming he did on his own behalf, or rather on the behalf of the peasant commune of which he was a part, and farming or other labour he did to meet his obligations to his master. These obligations were of two kinds: labour and money, and the relative weight of each depended on the type of estate and the inclinations of the landlord.

At one end of the scale, a landlord who had an abundance of fertile land and took a keen interest in farming would want to extract the maximum labour from his serfs, and might well waive entirely any money dues. Another landlord might have more serfs than he needed to work his own fields, in which case he would allow them, or some of them, to hire themselves out elsewhere for wages, demanding in return a fixed yearly sum. At the far end of the scale, a landlord might prefer not to farm at all, in which case he would turn the whole of his arable lands over to the serf commune, contenting himself with the profits from the sale of produce.

Such a system was obviously open to the grossest abuses, but to suggest that the general lot of the serfs was ceaseless toil punctuated by savage beatings would be wrong. An enlightened or even a prudent landlord, and there were many, would not wish to ruin his peasants. He would set feasible conditions of servitude, and as long as they were met he and his serfs would rub along amicably enough.

The serf would have a house for his family, a vegetable patch, a little bit of livestock and poultry, a share of the communal land and, since the landlord was in a sense responsible for his serfs, a degree of protection from any bullying or meddlesome officials.

In return for this he would provide, either himself or through his sons, an amount of labour that did not prevent him from attending to his own small farming operation. A serf in such conditions might well have viewed abstract concepts like freedom and liberty with indifference or downright scepticism, if, for example, he had compared his lot with that of a contemporary English farm labourer.

Nevertheless, in the manifold abuses of the institution of serfdom its fundamental immorality stands out blatantly. Many landlords were purely rapacious, and, if to meet their demands serfs were reduced to abject poverty, so be it. Others were absentees, enjoying the fleshpots of St. Petersburg or better yet Paris, and to pay for an extravagant life-style they would bring irresistible pressure to bear on their stewards to squeeze ever more revenue from their estates, regardless of the consequences. Some had no natural connection with their estates at all, but had bought them as pure investment, in which case they wanted the maximum return in the minimum time. Finally, not a few were sadistic brutes who despised the peasantry and saw it as their duty, or pleasure, to treat them in a sub-human fashion. Unwittingly, of course, they were creating a bedrock of unshakeable resentment that would soon find voice.

On becoming Tsar in 1856, Alexander II (right) embarked on a programme of social reform. Within a decade he had freed the serfs, remodelled the legal system, introduced a form of local government, created a free press and granted a measure of academic freedom to the universities.

In 1856, in the same year as his coronation (below), Alexander II made his momentous statement to the nobility of Moscow. 'It is better to abolish serfdom from above than to wait until it begins to abolish itself from below.'

peasant, by sad contrast, was notorious for his sloth, and left to his own devices would do the barest minimum to keep body and soul together. Without the discipline of the serf system he would actually slip backward from his existing level of poverty to utter destitution.

This pessimistic analysis was equally unsparing of the Russian landlord. His counterpart in England, it argued, could thrive in a competitive free market because he too was industrious and ambitious. He was keen to master new techniques for improved output and, as a consequence of generations of material advance, he had the capital to apply these techniques. The typical Russian landlord was not of a practical turn of mind and never had been, hence he had neither the skills nor the accrued captial to regenerate Russian agriculture along western lines.

The Tsar intervenes

Such a debate about the hypothetical effects of abolishing serfdom could have gone on forever had it not been for the intervention of the new Tsar, Alexander II. A rather weak man and by nature as conservative as his father Nicholas I, who died in despair towards the end of the Crimean War, Alexander nevertheless had a genuine insight into the serf

In March 1861 serfdom was abolished at a stroke. The text was distributed throughout the land, and, since virtually all peasants were illiterate, it was ordered to be read out in church (above), to ensure that every serf would fully understand the proposals.

Emancipation did little to improve the everyday life of the peasants. They were technically free, but still bound to the land. When they received land it was often smaller than the allotment they enjoyed under the serf system. Many left the land (right) to seek a living in the towns.

Debate over abolition

Enlightened thinkers in Russia had long favoured the abolition of serfdom, and not just on moral grounds. They argued that the progress of Western Europe showed, beyond doubt, that free labour was far more productive than slave or serf labour. Everywhere, agricultural progress had gone hand in hand with the demise of serfdom, and it was precisely because she clung to such an anachronism that Russia lagged so far behind her western neighbours — and was falling further behind all the time. Free the serfs and Russia would overnight shake off her medieval past and take her rightful place in the modern world — to the benefit of all classes of society.

Reactionary landlords, they stated, merely betrayed their ignorance of the outside world by claiming that such a transformation would impoverish them. The landed aristocracy in England were the richest and most powerful in the world, and serfdom there was a far distant memory. It was agricultural productivity that created genuine wealth for those who possessed land, not the ownership of a few hundred downtrodden serfs.

Against this was a conservative view held with equal tenacity. Russia, it was claimed, was not like western Europe, in fact she was not really a European nation at all, and it would therefore be folly to emulate western institutions in the naive assumption that western prosperity would automatically follow. The lower orders in such countries as England and Germany were well known for their industriousness, and for their desire to better their material lot. The Russian

Alexander II enlisted the help of the liberal intelligentsia to reform his regime. These university students and literary men soon became impatient with the slowness of true change in Russian society. But, though politically frustrated, many enjoyed a leisurely and relatively idyllic existence (left) – underlining the deep rift in Russian society.

In 1864 local councils were elected to deal with welfare, public health and education. The painting below shows peasants waiting patiently for aid outside the local administration offices.

question. Brushing aside any moral considerations, he considered the system historically doomed, and in April 1856 he stunned an assembly of the Moscow nobility with the trenchant observation: 'It is better to abolish serfdom from above than to wait until it begins to abolish itself from below.'

It was in the nature of Russian society that once the Tsar had expressed a sentiment, action would follow. He was an absolute monarch, not constrained by the need to carry even his most powerful subjects with him along any path he chose to tread. From the moment of his historic utterance, therefore, it was a foregone conclusion that serfdom was on its way out, and sooner rather than later. All that had to be decided were the terms for abolition.

The serf had to be released from his bondage, but in such a way that he was not uprooted from the land. Otherwise there would be chaos, with millions of peasants milling about uncontrolled, uncared for and confused about their new role in society, if indeed they had one. Therefore, the freed serf had to be given some land, land that could only come from its existing owners, either the proprietors, or the state. And since it was no one's intention, least of all the Tsar's, to impoverish the aristocracy, there would have to be compensation.

For the next few years the government wrestled with the problem, which boiled down to three main questions. How much land should the serf get? On what terms? How should the previous owner be compensated for his loss? The results of these lengthy deliberations finally emerged in 1861 in the form of an Imperial decree abolishing serf law with immediate effect. A manifesto spelling out the essentials of the new deal was distributed throughout the land, and in recognition of the illiteracy of the peasantry it was ordered that the manifesto be read out in church.

Given the complexity of the issues, and the potentially disastrous consequences of botching the job, the terms of the emancipation were ingeniously simple. The serfs were freed and given protection under the law. As far as possible, the land they received was the land they customarily used for their own purposes under serfdom, with the self-governing peasant commune stepping in to fill the void left by the landlord in matters of everyday management.

The peasant was to compensate his ex-master for the land he received, but indirectly. The state itself advanced the agreed sum to the dispossessed landlord, and was to recover the money in a series of annual payments from the peasant, the responsiblity for making the payment as well as taxes resting with the commune.

That was the essence of what can fairly be described as an unprecedented piece of social engineering. At a stroke 40 million serfs became free, and while the bargain struck to give them that freedom was heavily weighted in favour of the existing order, that it was achieved at all and implemented comparatively smoothly was a great accomplishment. After all, the attempt by that most progressive of nations, the United States, to rid itself of black slavery had at that very moment plunged America into a terrible civil war.

Equally remarkable was the speed with which other major reforms were triggered by the abolition of serfdom. Removing the jurisdiction of the landlords left huge gaps in the legal system, and it was duly overhauled along western lines – independent courts sitting openly, trial by jury in criminal cases, irremovable judges, all those legally progressive institutions which had been sadly lacking under the old order. And while it would be quite wrong to suggest that as a result of all this the serf suddenly took his place as an equal in society, even in the limited sense that a free-born English farm labourer of the time enjoyed equality, it was nevertheless a firm step away from the medieval past. So, too, was the establishment of a representative system of local government.

Reforms of the 1860s

The results of the reforms of the 1860s were necessarily mixed, for both classes were directly affected. Some proprietors seized on the opportunities presented by the sudden windfall of capital and overhauled their shrunken estates in line with advanced agricultural methods, using machinery and free labour to work the land more productively. Others proved incapable of adjusting to the new realities and sank into self-pitying torpor. Still others cut and run – delighted to be able to clear their debts, lease off the remainder of their estates to the peasants and flee rural boredom for the urban pleasures of St Petersburg or Moscow.

The consequences for the peasantry were no less varied. They were now free, for example, to marry whom they chose, and to work where they wanted, although here their freedom was circumscribed by their obligations to the commune. For a while the commune had exercised considerable authority over its members, mainly in such practical agricultural matters as what crop was to be grown at what time of

Peasants who left the land to work in the factories were obliged to send back some of their wages to the communal council. Living conditions in the cities were often no better than in the communes, and these metal workers in St Petersburg (below) lived in the rented corner of a single room.

Bildarchiv Preussischer Kulturbesitz

Novosti

In the 18th century Peter the Great (below) and Catherine the Great (below right) had turned Russia from its essentially Asian aspect to look westward into Europe. This only served to create a divide between the 'westernizers' and the 'slavophils' – those who saw Russia spiritually, and culturally, as a part of Asia.

year. Now the commune was responsible for seeing that the individual peasant paid his dues to the state. Hence the 'free' peasant could only obtain permission to leave the commune if he could satisfy his fellows that he would continue to pay his share – by sending back some of his wages, for instance, if he wanted to move off and work in a factory.

The reforms brought no guarantee, however, that the ex-serf would be materially better off than he had been before. Many, in fact, ended up with smaller allotments of land than they had enjoyed under serfdom, in which case they were still obliged to work hard and long for the old master – as hired labour rather then enforced labour, but with the same practical effect.

Westernizers versus slavophils

Tsar Alexander might have been forgiven for thinking that by resolving the central issue of the age, however imperfectly, he had set Russia on a steady course towards future strength and prosperity, and all without undermining the sacred principle of autocracy and the unique qualities of the Russian way of life. In fact, he had done nothing of the sort. What he had

done was to focus attention on the deep, some would say fathomless, divide in the Russian mind – a divide that went far beyond the immediate issue of reform to the nature of the Russian experience itself.

There existed side by side, and for quite some time, two diametrically opposed visions of what Russia was and where her destiny lay. Two of the 18th century's most forceful monarchs, Peter the Great and Catherine the Great, had virtually frogmarched Russia from its Asian past into what they saw as its European future. Peter had built his magnificent new capital on the western frontier of his empire, so as to provide 'a window by which the Russians might look into civilized Europe'. Like Peter himself, who was nearly seven feet tall, St Petersburg was built on a colossal scale: immense palaces, public buildings and churches, vast squares and avenues, and all of it inspired by Peter's vision of what Russia should aspire to.

Under Catherine, the Europeanization of the Russian aristocracy reached its zenith. Anyone with pretensions to being civilized spoke French fluently, and in preference to Russian, aped French fashions and extolled the merits of French classical literature; in short, a cultivated Russian put up as high a barrier as he could between himself and what he viewed as the semi-barbarous society that he had been born into.

It is easy to mock such affectation, but underlying it was a serious assumption: namely that Russia's past was an unenviable one and that a great future was hers only if she could become thoroughly westernized from the top down. And it was this underlying assumption, rather than the posturings of a few overly-refined courtiers, that exposed those who were westernized to attacks from a rival school of thinkers, the so-called 'slavophils'.

Based mainly on the older pre-St Petersburg capital of Moscow, the slavophils looked at Russia and Russian history through the other end of the telescope. As they saw it, things had been going well enough until Peter the Great came along with his mad vision of westernization. Russia was geographically, spiritually and culturally an eastern, not a western, society.

Attempts to assassinate Alexander II were made in 1866, 1873, and in 1880. Finally on 13 March 1881, the terrorists achieved their aim. A bomb was thrown as the Tsar's carriage passed along the Catherine Canal (below). He was unharmed but as he attempted to comfort his wounded guards a second, fatal bomb fell at his feet (below right).

Chris Barker

They considered that the principle of autocracy, with all power resting securely in the hands of the anointed Tsar, had saved Russia from the political upheavals and class struggles that had proved such a disfiguring feature of western life. Russia had been blessed with the Orthodox religion and thus spared the great Roman Catholic/Protestant schism that had overshadowed western Europe for centuries.

Tragically, they thought, large segments of the upper classes had been beguiled by the siren song of western materialism – the mania for progress at any cost, the flirtation with liberalism and the cult of the individual. But the peasantry, even after emancipation, were still mercifully untainted, and it was to them that the slavophils looked for a regeneration of traditional Russian values.

The young radicals

The long-standing rift between westernizers and slavophils began to take on a new dimension during and after the reform era of the 1860s. A new set of western ideas was thrown into the intellectual and political arena. These were radical notions which were as abhorrent to the cultured aristocrats as they were to diehard slavophils. The advocates of these new ideas were mainly young university-educated idealists, who believed that the reforms had gone nowhere near far enough, indeed were no more than a swindle since they left power and money with the few while the majority remained in abject poverty. The complete transformation of society was their aim, a true egalitarianism based on the natural socialism of the peasant commune.

During the 1860s small revolutionary groups began to appear. The outstanding figure was N. G. Chernyshevsky (above), a socialist writer, who was to influence a generation of young Russians.

The 1870s saw a revival of revolutionary activity – and a revival of harsh counter-measures enforced by military power (above left).

Their Utopian dream appeared as a hideous nightmare to all the established forces in Russian society, and the reaction set in swiftly. The authorities began cracking down heavily on the universities and on the press which disseminated radical thought. This had the predictable effect of goading the young radicals into greater defiance, both open and clandestine, and in 1866 there was the first of a succession of attempts on Alexander's life.

It was, of course, ironic that the 'Tsar Liberator' should become the focus of the radicals' hatred, since he himself had played midwife to the reform movement in the first place. Now, however, he began to take refuge in more traditional beliefs. The principles of autocracy and the established order were sacred to him, and the violent attack upon them – and upon his own person – showed that reform had gone far enough, if not too far already. It was time to call a halt, time to bring the nation to heel.

So began the era of the exile, the secret society and the bomb. Many of the radicals fled to the relative sanctuary of western Europe, mostly to Switzerland, and from there conducted a tireless war of words against the Russian state. Those who remained behind organized themselves into various secret societies,

reflecting different shades of opinion about how to bring down the established order. And from within and without Russia endless terrorist plots were hatched, and not a few brought to deadly fruition.

The real target, however, remained Alexander himself, and on 13 March 1881, the terrorists finally achieved their aim. As the Tsar was driving along the Catherine Canal in St Petersburg a bomb was thrown at his carriage. He was unharmed, and got out of the carriage to comfort some of his Cossack guards who had been injured. Then a second assassin lobbed a bomb between his feet, which mutilated him dreadfully. He had time only to murmur 'Home to the palace, to die there', before he died.

The assassination of Alexander shocked Russia profoundly, and it widened even further the gulf between those who wanted more reforms whether of a liberal or revolutionary nature, and those who saw national salvation only through repression. The new Tsar, Alexander III, brought little comfort to progressives of any nature. The great Russian experiment – the attempt to achieve social and political harmony from above – had failed. The train of events that would culminate in the revolution of 1917 had been set firmly in motion.

After the death of Alexander II and the crowning of Alexander III (below) came the rejection of any plans to introduce elected representatives into the government structure. The re-establishment of virtual dictatorship succeeded in fermenting the revolutionary ideals that would explode in the Bolshevik revolution of 1917.

IN THE BACKGROUND

Literature in Russia

The Classical Ballet

Despite the reforms of Alexander II, 19th-century Russia was governed by a despotic and authoritarian regime. The Tsars' absolute monarchy was upheld by a large force of secret police which monitored the activities of artists and intellectuals. Despite – or perhaps because of – this repression, the 19th century was a time of great intellectual and cultural ferment in Russia, when writers like Pushkin, Lermontov, Turgenev, Dostoyevsky and Tolstoy produced some of the greatest works of Russian, if not world, literature. Their achievements in the novel and poetry were paralleled in dance by the Russian ballet, which brought the art – begun in Renaissance Italy and developed in France – to its peak of classical perfection. This tradition has continued, and in the Bolshoi and Kirov Ballets, the Soviet Union has two of the greatest companies in the world.

'A mirror of society'

The lives of the brilliant and varied collection of characters who inhabit the world of Russian literature are hardly more colourful than those of the great writers who created them.

W. Schwarz 'The Tsarina's Spring Pilgrimage, 1868'. Tretyakov Gallery, Moscow/Bildarchiv Preussischer Kulturbesitz

The fashionable, wealthy upper classes promenade in front of the Moscow Kremlin in 1839 (above). Heavily influenced by the West, the custom and style of their lives contrast starkly with those of the peasants. This divided society is a theme much explored by the novelists of the period. It is clearly expressed (left) as the richly gilded and exotic sleighs of the Tsarina sweep through the countryside, past the drab hovels of a peasant community.

Russian literature between 1830 and 1880 can take its place as one of the major artistic achievements of European civilization. And yet all the works were written by people who came to maturity in Russia when it was one of the least socially developed countries in Europe.

Despotic tsarist regimes, sustained by a feudal peasant system, savagely and often arbitrarily censored the free expression of ideas. A large secret police force existed to monitor the activities of writer and intellectuals, and at the word of the authorities 'dissidents' were exiled on the slightest suspicion to the provinces, the Caucasus or Siberia.

Perhaps, paradoxically, it was this repression which stimulated the writers into questioning the world in which they lived, which can be seen as the basic story of the Russian novel. By concentrating on the events, people and ordinary landscapes of life, 19th-century Russian novelists freed the language and the subject matter of the novel from the stiffness and artificiality of the 18th century.

Novels from the latter half of the 19th century must be viewed in the light of the great intellectual ferments that began in the 1840s. In this decade a radical intelligentsia arose in which dissident members of the nobility mingled with a new class of men. The 'new' men, often journalists, came from humble backgrounds but this no longer prevented them from acquiring education.

Despite the existence of censorship and the activities of the secret police, it was an era of intense questioning of the established order. The 'progressives' of the 1840s looked to western Europe as the model for constitutional freedoms both for the individual and for the peasant class as a whole, which was oppressed in Russia as nowhere else in Europe. To this group, known as the 'westerners', belonged many critics, poets and writers including Turgenev and Dostoyevsky.

A different group, the Slavophiles, also opposed the established order, but looked for an answer to the nation's problems in a vision of a return to the 'Old Russia' which had preceded the Europeanizing reforms of Peter the Great (1682–1725). To the Slavophiles it seemed that the Russian people, with their traditional ways and values and their unquestioning faith in a mystical Orthodoxy, represented a slumbering giant which could restore

direction to a Russia which had lost its way. Some members of the Western group, notably Dostoyevsky, later turned to Slavophilism.

Alexander Pushkin (1799–1837)

The first of the great Russian novelists, Pushkin, was primarily a poet. His lyrical and narrative poems are the peaks of his versatile output which included spare, forceful prose tales, dramatic and historical writings, epigrams and criticism. Using the Russian language more flexibly and combining this with the classic novelist's virtues of economy, elegance and wit, he fascinated the reading classes of 19th century Russia and became a source of inspiration for many other writers.

Aristocratically born, he left his academy in 1817 for an undemanding post in government service in the Russian capital, St Petersburg. There he moved in a circle of dissipated young noblemen. He acquired a reputation for brilliant radical verses and in 1820 was exiled for three years to the south of Russia, where he travelled first to the Caucasus, then the Crimea and then to Kishinev in the south-west.

In 1824, he was moved to Odessa, but after an ill-advised love affair he was exiled again, this time to his family estate in north-west Russia where he remained under the close surveillance of the authorities. His historic drama, *Boris Godunov*, belongs to this period.

After the death of Tsar Alexander I in 1825, friends interceded on Pushkin's behalf with the new emperor, Nicholas. In a show of clemency the emperor received Pushkin back at court as Russia's greatest poet. However, thus established he found himself under a stricter censorship than before and his movements were greatly restricted.

At first he wrote little, but in the 1830s he completed his masterly narrative poem *Eugene Onegin*, a number of prose tales, including *The Queen of Spades*, some tragedies, a few short poems,

The Captain's Daughter (a short historical novel) as well as the poem, *The Bronze Horseman*.

In 1831 he married a young beauty who became addicted to the life of the court. Financial difficulties and worries about her improprieties weighed him down. At the end of 1836 rumours of a scandal concerning his wife provoked him to challenge a French officer in the Russian service to a duel; Pushkin was shot and died two days later.

The work of Pushkin's that has had the greatest influence on later writers was *Eugene Onegin*. Told in 14-line stanzas, the story is about a young Byronic hero, Eugene, who, wearying of life in St Petersburg, goes to a country estate which he is to inherit. There he meets the artless and romantic Tatyana, daughter

Many of the novelists of the period viewed the peasant classes as the true representatives of the Russian character. The honesty and lack of veneer in the lives of the peasants (below) is compared with the sophistication of the upper classes.

Novosti

During his exile in the south of Russia, Alexander Pushkin (left), first of the great Russian novelists, read and was influenced by Byron's narrative poems. The hero of Eugene Onegin, Pushkin's dramatic poem, owes his nature as a talented but bored, embittered young man, to this source.

Years after his rejection of Tatyana (below) Eugene Onegin returns to have the tables turned on him. Not only did this dramatic poem influence writers but it also had its impact on other artists. Tchaikovsky used the theme for his opera Eugene Onegin.

people. In 1841 he fought another duel with a fellow officer, over a woman, and was killed instantly.

Nikolay Gogol (1809–52)

Gogol was born in the Ukraine into the small gentry class. He obtained a post as a government clerk in St Petersburg in 1828. He relieved his loneliness by writing colourful tales of his native region. These met with success one of them being his historical romance, *Taras Bulba,* published in 1835. He was introduced to literary circles, where he met Pushkin who gave him the ideas for his two great works, the play, *The Government Inspector* (1836) and the novel *Dead Souls* (1842). These works are historical portraits of provincial characters and society. Both are handled with such gusto and range of comic technique that they induce fondness for, rather than mockery of, their subjects.

In *Dead Souls,* Chichikov, a needy nobleman embarks on fraud. Landlords in Russia were required to pay tax on the number of serfs (or 'souls') they owned. Chichikov purchases from a number of land-owners their liabilities for 'souls' who have died since the last census. He registers them as settled on remote estates of his own and raises finance mortgage for himself using the 'dead souls' as surety. The comic exuberance of Gogol's prose is over-

of a local worthy. She falls desperately in love with Onegin, but he rejects her. Tricked by a young poet friend into attending a ball in Tatyana's honour, Eugene in revenge sets himself at the poet's sweet-heart. A duel follows in which the poet is killed; Eugene departs for foreign travel. When he returns to Moscow he is amazed to find Tatyana married to a prince and transformed into a remarkable woman. The tables are turned on him: he becomes besotted with her, but she rejects him. Her speech to him concludes with some of the most famous lines in Russian poetry:

I love you (why should I dissemble?)
But I became another's wife;
I shall be true to him through life.

Eugene Onegin influenced later writers not only because of the use of a Byronic hero and a noble heroine, but by the demonstration that the choice of significant detail could create a scene in a few words and so add a sense of realism to the narrative. While conjuring up the physical setting of the tale, Pushkin also conveyed brilliantly the details of social events using telling snatches of overheard conversation.

Mikhail Lermontov 1814–41

Lermontov was born into an aristocratic family and was principally a poet. He had begun writing and reading verse, and developing an interest in Byron since the age of 13, but it was not until 1837, when he wrote a poem on the death of Pushkin that he acquired a literary reputation. In the poem, he blamed the court for Pushkin's death, and as a result was exiled for a year to do military service in the Caucasus.

He was pardoned in 1838 and returned to St Petersburg. Although he did not mix much in literary circles he was able to get his poems published and in 1840 his novel *A Hero of Our Time* was published. In the same year he fought a duel, which both men survived but for which he was again exiled to the Caucasus. He served with bravery in military expeditions against the fierce Chechen mountain

whelming and his place in Russian literature is unique.

Gogol did not attempt psychological analysis nor did he ultimately, question the society in which he lived; nevertheless he widened the possibilities for realism in the novel, building his characters through small details in a way no previous writers had done.

Gogol was taken up by the radical intellectuals of the 1840s, who, emphasizing his satirical vein, interpreted his work as an indictment of Russian society. This was not Gogol's intention and he was later sharply rejected by the radicals. He spent his last years abroad unhappily and died in a state of religious mania and depression.

Ivan Turgenev (1818–83)

Although he was an intelligent sympathizer of the radical cause, Turgenev was a literary man, rather than a revolutionary, and his novels show the classic virtues of restraint and grace.

Born into the gentry, he was educated at the universities of St Petersburg, Moscow and Berlin, where he took up western philosophical ideals. When he returned to Russia he attempted careers in the academic world and in government service, before, in 1845, turning to writing. Between 1847 and 1851 he wrote a series of short stories based on hunting incidents. Displaying a sensitive appreciation of the rural scene, they also contained incidents involving serfs and landowners.

When collected and published in 1852 as *A Sportsman's Notebook* the radical intellectuals seized on the book as a major piece of social criticism and Turgenev achieved instant fame. This alarmed the authorities who on a pretext exiled him for a while to his mother's estate.

His first novels, *Rudin* (1856), *A Nest of Gentlefolk* (1859), and *On the Eve* (1860) sustained his reputation, but the reaction of the radicals to his fourth novel, *Father and Sons* (1862), disappointed him. He left Russia and lived abroad, mixing mainly in French literary circles. His later novels were felt in Russia to be out of touch with the times, though he

Novosti

continued to be well-regarded in France.

A central theme of Turgenev's writing up to 1862 was that of the desirability, but difficulty, of being a man of action. In a short story published in 1850, Turgenev gave the catchphrase 'a superfluous man' to Russian literature. This phrase describes a stereotype who represents the ineffectual idealist, the sort of person who talks much but is unable to act. The heroes of each of his first four novels are such people. These novels are all set in a sort of vacuum in the countryside, the same milieu he used in his play *A Month in the Country*. In these novels a love affair between a would-be man of action and a strong heroine (the latter owing something to

Mikhail Lermontov (left) author of A Hero Of Our Time. *Told in several episodes this is the portrait of the brilliant but destructive Pechorin. He marries the daughter of a Caucasian chief. An enraged rival abducts and murders the girl (top left). Another episode deals with Pechorin's churlish treatment of his friend Maxim (top right). At a spa, Pechorin idly trifles with the affections of a princess (below left). In the inevitable duel his friend, Grushnitsky, is killed. The last story (below right) is about a fellow-officer, Vulich, who survives a game of Russian roulette, only to be killed a few hours later by a mad Cossack.*

I. E. Repin 'The Cossacks' Letter'. Archiv für Kunst und Geschichte

Society for Cultural Relation with the USSR

Pushkin's Tatyana) is described brilliantly.

The heroes of the first three novels are seen to fail; but with Bazarov, the hero of *Fathers and Sons* (Turgenev's best-known work), he felt that he had succeeded at last in depicting a strong man. Bazarov, nihilistic, materialistic and owing something to the Byronic model, is the 'Angry Young Man' of his day. The portrait Turgenev painted alarmed conservative circles and outraged the radicals, who found it lacking in humanity. It is, in fact, the peak of his social observations and is a delicate study of relationships within a small group of people.

The description, in *Fathers and Sons,* of the uncle of a friend with whom Bazarov comes to stay, exhibits Turgenev's power to outline character through telling details. The uncle, we learn, keeps up appearances, although middle-aged and living in the country, well away from society:

His close-cropped grey hair had the black sheen of unpolished silver; his face, the colour of old ivory but without a wrinkle, had unusually regular and clean-cut features as though carved by a sharp and delicate chisel, and showed traces of remarkable beauty: particularly fine were his clear dark almond-shaped eyes . . . Drawing from his trouser pocket an exquisite hand having long tapering pink nails – a hand whose beauty was further enhanced by the snowy whiteness of his cuff buttoned with a single opal – Pavel Petrovich held it out to his nephew. After a preliminary European handshake he kissed Arkady three times in the Russian fashion, that is to say, he touched his cheeks thrice with his perfumed moustaches, and murmured 'Welcome home.'

Fyodor Dostoyevsky (1821–81)

Dostoyevsky after a gloomy, restricted childhood in Moscow, then trained as a military engineer. He resigned his commission in 1844 in order to devote himself to writing. His first novel, *Poor Folk,* combining something of Gogol's grotesque naturalism with a deep pity for the downtrodden,

Society for Cultural Relation with the USSR

Mauro Pucciarelli

A scene from The Government Inspector by Gogol (above). The play rests on the exposure of the inefficient and stupid behaviour of provincial officials. They mistake a feather-brained young man for a government inspector, travelling incognito. The play ends with the arrival of the real inspector. Although the play was well-received it produced 'a depressing effect' on its author Nikolay Gogol (left).

appeared in 1846 and was hailed as a great event by radical critics. His subsequent stories did not receive the same attention and although he remained a radical he ceased to associate with literary circles. In 1849 he was among a group of socialists arrested and imprisoned in the St Peter and Paul Fortress to await trial. In December 1849 they were led out, told they were sentenced to death, and made to watch the preparations to shoot the first three of them. At the last moment a messenger came from the court with 'a reprieve'. In fact this was all a cruel joke: they had not been sentenced to death but to prison. Dostoyevsky was a prisoner in Siberia for four years and then served as a common soldier for another four. While in prison he experienced a profound religious crisis and in outlook changed from a 'Westerner' to a Slavophile.

In 1857 he married and in 1859 was allowed to return to St Petersburg. He plunged into a world of journalism that was heady with notions of reform, following the accession of Tsar Alexander II in 1855. With his brother Michael, Dostoyevsky began a review which was a success until suppressed in 1863 (owing to a mistaken reading by the censors). Another journal was begun in 1864, but Dostoyevsky's wife and brother both died soon afterwards and, with his brother's family to look after as well, he found himself bankrupt. To meet his liabilities he produced in frantic haste his first major novel, *Crime and Punishment* (1865–66). In 1867 he married his short-hand secretary and they left Russia for four years until his finances had recovered sufficiently to enable him to return. Then followed *The Idiot* (1868), *The Possessed* (1871–72) and he began making plans for another novel which was eventually to become *The Brothers Karamazov* (1880). After his return to Russia, Dostoyevsky's fortunes improved and he ended his life a famous man.

His four great novels are melodramatic in the extreme, full of suspense and seemingly irrational

I. Levitan 'Spring High Water'. Novosti

Novosti

Ivan Turgenev (left), whose works are decribed on pages 89-90, was born in Paris and studied at the universities of Moscow, St Petersburg and Berlin. While a child he grew to love the Russian countryside, since it was here he took refuge from an unhappy home, dominated by his strong-willed mother. This affection is reflected in the poetic settings of his novels (above).

events which yet have a strange logic about them. Drawing on a wide range of characters from all strata of society, Dostoyevsky plunges the reader into a violent world of murders, sickness, hallucinations and dreams as well as of extremes of vice and saintliness. He excels in dealing with the underworld – both that of society and that of the mind. It is a fluid, unstable, essentially tragic world. *Crime and Punishment* has perhaps the greatest unity of plot. Raskolnikov, the central figure, persuades himself that he has the right to place himself above the normal constraints of right and wrong, and kills and robs an elderly woman, a pawnbroker. The novel takes us grippingly through the act, and then, into an exploration of Raskolnikov's mind, revealing to him aspects that were previously unknown to him and which finally force him to redeem himself by confessing the crime to a young prostitute who loves him. With psychological insight Dostoyevsky creates a policeman who guesses Raskolnikov's guilt, but who waits, luring the criminal into a voluntary second confession.

Dostoyevsky's narrative mastery can be seen in an uncanny episode which precedes the murder. Raskolnikov, having made his first visit to the pawnbroker to pawn a ring, and taking a great dislike to her goes to a tavern. Here he chances to overhear a conversation about the pawnbroker, in which one of the speakers argues that it would be justice if the woman were to be murdered and her money devoted to 'the service of humanity'.

Raskolnikov was violently agitated. Of course, it was all ordinary youthful talk and thought such as he had often heard before in different forms and on different themes. But why had he happened to hear such a discussion and such ideas at the very moment when his own brain was just conceiving . . . the very same ideas? And why, just at the moment when he had brought away the embryo of his idea from the old woman, had he dropped at once upon a conversation with her? This coincidence always seemed strange to him. This trivial talk in a tavern had an immense influence on him in his later action; as though there had really been in it something preordained, some guiding hint . . .

Leo Tolstoy (1828–1910)

Born of an ancient aristocratic family, Tolstoy was reared in an atmosphere of cultivated wealth. Endowed with a great humanitarian instinct, he abandoned his university studies to try to improve the conditions of the serfs on the estates he had inherited. Frustrated by their apathy he joined, in 1851, a line regiment serving in the Caucasus. Here he wrote his autobiographical *Childhood,* published in *The Contemporary* in 1852, which immediately made his name in literary circles. Even in this early work, and its companion volumes of the 1850s, *Boyhood* and *Youth,* Tolstoy's combination of *joie-de-vivre* and sharp, moralizing intelligence can be seen. His rendering of the pains and pleasures of

The Battle of Borodino (right) followed by the fall of Moscow to the invading Napoleonic army is one of the momentous historical events which Tolstoy used in War and Peace, *as the background for the lives and loves of his characters. All of the lives involved are changed dramatically by the outcome of events.*

It was while Dostoyevsky (right) was in exile in Siberia that the idea for his first great novel, Crime and Punishment, *came to him. Raskolnikov (far right), the hero of the novel, sits alone in his dingy room, contemplating the murder of the pawnbroker.*

A page from the manuscript of The Possessed *(below), also by Dostoyevsky, published in 1872.*

Society for Cultural Relation with the USSR

Novosti

Mauro Pucciarelli

A religious procession in the Kursk district (right). The blind faith of the common people in the mystic tradition of the Orthodox church led many Russian thinkers and writers to see it as a source of regeneration. Dostoyevsky, for one, had a messianic vision of the destiny of 'Holy Russia'.

Repin 'Religious Procession in the Kursk District'. Novosti

Lejeune 'Battle of Moscow'. Versailles/Bulloz

growing up already shows his meticulous attention to detail.

In the Caucasus too he began *The Cossacks* (published in 1863), a hymn to the naturalness and unconscious zest for life of the Cossack people. At his own request he served in the bitterly fought Crimean campaign, and the anti-heroic reportage of his *Sebastopol Sketches* (1855–56) brought him further notice. After leaving the army, he led a dissipated life in St Petersburg for a while. Here he met members of the literary intelligentsia but found himself out of sympathy with their politics. Between 1857 and 1862 Tolstoy alternately travelled abroad and conducted educational experiments with the peasants on his estates. In 1862 he married, and his wife Sofya proved the ideal partner for a literary landed gentleman, providing him for the next 15 years with a stable home, a family and secretarial assistance.

In these years he produced his two great masterpieces, *War and Peace* (begun in 1863 and published 1865–69) and *Anna Karenina* (1873–77). In the late 1870s, however, he underwent a spiritual crisis and devoted himself to moralistic and pacifist writings. Although at first he renounced his art, he did in fact produce some major works including *The Death of Ivan Ilyich* (1886), *Resurrection* (1899), *Hadji Murad* (1901–04) and a play, *The Power of Darkness* (1886). But these are starker, more sombre works. When he died at an obscure railway

Novosti

Natasha (above), the spirited heroine of War and Peace, embraces her childhood sweetheart, Boris.

The first fateful encounter (right) of Vronsky and Anna, central characters in Anna Karenina.

Novosti

station in 1910, after an undignified flight from his wife, he had been a world-famous figure, as a pacifist, for a decade.

In *War and Peace,* Tolstoy created a national epic. Set against the ebb and flow of the Napoleonic wars, and culminating in Napoleon's defeat after the battle of Borodino in 1812, it seems to depict the entire life of Russia, from tsar to peasant. Overwhelmingly the novel illustrates the futility and wastefulness of war — the sad, squalid, pitiful reality of soldiers fighting soldiers — so much at odds with the glowing accounts, as of a large-scale chess game, that reached the people back home.

The central characters among the men, Prince Andrey and Pierre Bezukhov, are rounded portraits without being, as nearly all Tolstoy's protagonists had been hitherto, thinly disguised autobiographical projections. The Rostov family, too, are key figures in the book, symbolizing a naturalness which Tolstoy so much admired — and envied. None of the Rostovs is so full of vitality as Natasha, one of the most marvellous heroines in fiction, and whose realization was a significant advance for Tolstoy in the creation of female characters. Here he shows the breathlessness of Natasha aged 16, at her first ball:

She could only grasp all that awaited her when, walking over the red cloth, she went into the vestibule, took off her cloak and walked beside Sonya in front of her mother between the flowers up the lighted staircase. Only then she remembered how she must behave at a ball, and tried to assume the majestic manner that she considered indispensible for a girl at a ball. But luckily she felt that there was a mist before her eyes; she could see nothing clearly, her pulse beat a hundred times a minute, and the blood throbbed at her heart. She was unable to assume the manner that would have made her absurd; and moved on, thrilling with

excitement, and trying with all her might simply to conceal it. And it was just in this mood that she looked her best.

While painting on the widest possible canvas, Tolstoy employed to the full the techniques of significant physical and psychological detail which had already appeared in *Childhood.* The details observed are often trivial or mundane — a particular way of turning the head, or an habitual gesture. In Tolstoy's art they function as the creators of character and mood in the novel. Another technique is the description of a particular person or incident through the eyes of a number of different characters or groups of people. The effect is that of a solid picture of real life.

With *Anna Karenina* Tolstoy employed the same techniques to produce a vast study of contemporary life in Russia. The tragic tale of the love affair between the dashing Vronsky and Anna, the beautiful wife of a high-ranking civil servant, who ends her life when it has ceased to hold any meaning for her, is counterbalanced by the story of Levin's search for meaning in life and his courtship and marriage of the princess, Kitty Scherbatsky.

The famous opening lines of *Anna Karenina* plunge the reader (after the manner of Pushkin, a great influence on Tolstoy) into the main theme of the novel:

All happy families resemble one another, but each unhappy family is unhappy in its own way.

While affirming the goodness of life as strongly as he did in *War and Peace,* Tolstoy leaves Levin's moral quest in *Anna Karenina* unresolved. As in all his greatest works Tolstoy provides the reader with the sensation of living rather than reading the story. *Anna Karenina* is perhaps Russia's greatest contribution to literature.

Although in his youth he was fairly dissolute, in the last 30 years of his life, Tolstoy became moralistic and pacifist. During this time his day-to-day involvement with the lives and work of the peasants on his estates grew, and he adopted peasant dress (right). In a work published in 1898, What is art?, he stated that all his earlier work was worthless. He renounced his copyright on work published after 1881 and divided his property up between his wife and nine children. His wife, however, did not accept his new philosophies and the rift between them grew until, aged 82, he fled from his home.

Mauro Pucciarelli

'Pas de gloire'

With the spectacular festivals of the Italian Renaissance the seeds of ballet were sown. Over the centuries to come the art flowered into one of the most graceful and dazzling theatrical entertainments.

The legendary Le Pas de Quatre (1845) *united four of the outstanding ballerinas of the Romantic era – Marie Taglioni, Carlotta Grisi, Lucile Grahn and Fanny Cerrito. No other single spectacle captured so completely the spirit of Romantic ballet. This was the hey-day of the ballerina – an ethereal spirit from another world, delicately poised on point, crowned with flowers, and clad in floating white tulle.*

Two elaborate costume designs by Bernardo Buontalenti (right) for an intermezzo *(between-scene entertainment) presented in Florence in 1589. They are infused with the spirit of antiquity and Renaissance pageantry.*

The ballet de cour *(court ballet) was central to the festivities of the court of Savoy in Turin. This allegorical set (1647), with its flaming city backdrop, is designed to complement the fantastic dancing figure on the stage (below). He personifies one of the four humours, or temperaments – the fiery, passionate, choleric disposition.*

Attilio Bigo Collection/Hamlyn Picture Library

The magical ballets of Tchaikovsky, which represent a pinnacle in the history of ballet, have a fascinating and glittering history. Ballet first flowered in Italy, in the magnificent courts of the High Renaissance, where dance was one of the social graces exhibited by the nobility. Indeed, for a long time to come, dance would be primarily the bodily demonstration of polite behaviour. So much so, that in the 15th century, dancing masters became important figures in the Italian courts. They instructed their charges in dress and deportment, and taught them the many individual dance forms of the day. At the time, costumes were long and full. Dances were variations on the act of walking with grace. They were stately and thoroughly dignified.

The spectacular entertainments popular in the courts of the Renaissance also placed great emphasis on dance, amid artistic collaborations of poetry, music, song, pageant, décor and costumes. With the new revival of interest in the civilization of classical times, they usually dealt with themes from the mythology of Greece and Rome on an extraordinarily lavish scale.

The Ballet de Cour
If Italy saw the greatest dance performances of the High Renaissance, France was the first nation to imitate such spectacles. Catherine de Medici

Fotomas Index

1519–89), Italian wife to the French King Henri II, enjoyed the arts and used them to celebrate the political status quo. In this she encouraged and employed both French and Italian artists at her court – such as the Italian dancing-master Baldassarino del Belgioso, called Balthasar de Beaujoyeux. It was Beaujoyeux who organized the famous *Ballet Comique de la Reine Louise* in 1581. At this time, Catherine was the Dowager Queen and her third son, Henri III, was King. Catherine commissioned the ballet in honour of his wife's sister's wedding. Lasting five hours, it was staged in a vast hall in the palace of the Louvre, the audience of several thousands seated on three sides. Music, scenery, costumes, machinery, poetry, recitation – all were intermingled with the dancing with such skill that the event became famous world-wide. It told the story of man's liberation from the enchantress Circe – the implication for the audience being that the French nation was being similarly delivered from danger by the benevolent French monarchy. Henri's young Queen, Louise, and her sister, the bride, took part.

That was the first *Ballet de cour,* or court ballet. Performances of this type flourished in the decades that followed, especially under the first Bourbon monarchs of France – Henri IV, his son Louis XIII and his son Louis XIV (1638–1715). It was in the *Ballet de la Nuit* in 1653 that the last king, then just an

adolescent, appeared as the resplendent sun and so gained the title *Le Roi Soleil* or the Sun King.

Yet during those years dance declined as an art for members of the court. And so in 1661 Louis, in his concern to 're-establish the dance in its true perfection', set up the Académie Royale de Danse (Royal Academy of Dance). The purpose of this institution was to codify rules and precepts for dance and its teaching: but the 13 dancing-masters who were employed by the Academy were overawed by the surroundings of the Louvre Palace in which they had been given an official room and preferred to meet in a tavern instead! They achieved very little on behalf of the Academy.

In the same year the king's treasurer Fouquet, opening his new and magnificent palace at Vaux-le-Vicomte with an extended fête to entertain the king, presented *Les Fâcheux.* The great writer of French comedy Molière had been asked to organize both a ballet and a play, but by this point the shortage of good dancers was so marked that he decided to place sections of the ballet between scenes of his play so as to give the dancers time to change costumes. Fouquet's lavish expenditure on the fête, however, so shocked the king that it led to the minister's downfall; but *Les Fâcheux,* the first comédie-ballet, delighted him. It became the model for a series of such entertainments involving Moliere, the composer Jean-

The young Louis XIV appeared in **Le Ballet de la Nuit** *(1653), resplendent in his role as the Sun King (above left). His stunning costume created a tremendous impact and earned him the title of 'Le Roi Soleil'.*

Jacques Callot's engraving (above) crystallizes a moment from the ballet **La Liberazione di Tirrenio,** *performed in Florence in 1616. The dancers inhabit three different worlds – appearing on the floor, on a platform stage behind, and beyond, in the far distance, in 'cloud machines' above the stage. Note the way in which the dancers are surrounded by the audience.*

Marie Camargo (left) was a lively and brilliant dancer, who managed steps which had previously seemed beyond the capabilities of a female performer.

*Boydell's satirical engraving (below left) savagely ridicules the empty posturing of the **ballet tragique** this mime scene from Medée et Jason (1781) the gre and conceited Gaetano Vestris woefully overacts, gestures made all the more ludicrous by his completely inappropriate costume.*

Baptiste Lully and the choreographer Pier Beauchamps. This led to Lully's opera-ballets, whe the spoken drama of Molière was replaced by tra opera – a form which contained about one quar ballet. In 1699 the Académie Royale de Musique – Paris Opéra – was founded, with Lully at its head.

The professional dancer takes the stage

But now another change took place, one which wou permanently affect the whole nature of theatri dancing. Despite the encouragement and example King Louis, himself a fine and enthusiastic dancer, fe courtiers were keen or good at the art themselv Because of this, in 1672 a new school was attached the Opéra, to train professional dancers for the ope ballets. Now, for the first time, professional dance began to take centre stage in leading roles, replaci the aristocracy: they were trained in dance as a mirr of the deportment and manners of the nobles. Th vertical carriage of the courtiers and their elega turn-out of the legs from the hips served as a model f the dancers. In this style dances were planned alo careful and elaborate floor-patterns: and the need f precision in footwork became apparent, so th

positions of the feet – five particular positions – were codified. Previously social dance and theatrical dance had been very similar in form; now a gap between the two began to develop. The change was marked by the move of theatrical dance from an open hall to a stage behind a proscenium arch – away from the spectators, no longer in their midst.

A male domain

At this time men alone danced onstage in splendid isolation. But, in 1681, four female dancers, led by Mademoiselle Lafontaine, broke their monopoly. However, the difference between the two sexes' style of dance and costume reflected their place in the social balance. The women, their legs covered by long, heavy dresses, were graceful and decorative, but the men were more mobile and active, displaying vigour as well as elegance. The male dancers were in the vanguard of technical development. Led by such stars as Jean Balon and Louis Dupré, they introduced escalating feats of jumping *(elevation)*, beaten steps in which the legs and feet beat or intercrossed in the air *(cabrioles, entrechats)*, and turning *(pirouettes)*. But the dancers at the court of France retained their aristocratic composure. Elegant style more than brilliance became the hallmark of Paris-trained performers.

This was also the era of the three genres or 'types'. According to physique, dancers were trained in different techniques – noble or *sérieux* for tall, well-formed dancers who excelled in dignified, slow, controlled movements; *demi-caractère* for dancers of a more lively and less refined bent; and the *comique* or *grotesque* dancers, for those who performed character parts or national dances. This carefully stratified system brought dancing to a new level of sophistication, making it a worthy representative of this 'Age of Reason and Technique', as the 18th century has been called.

The ballet d'action

This century was also marked by a new concern with ballet as a self-sufficient vehicle for drama. The man who did most to proclaim this cause was Jean-Georges Noverre (1727–1810). The career of this great choreographer, teacher and writer was punctuated throughout by struggle against reactionary influences, a struggle which was often made more bitter by his fiery, arrogant, proud temperament. He achieved recognition in 1754 when *Les Fêtes Chinoises* was staged in Paris – a picturesque and entrancing representation of a Chinese festival. Its popular success was so immense that the English actor-manager David Garrick invited him to stage it at the Theatre Royal, Covent Garden. The result was just as memorable – but in quite a different way. France and Britain were on the brink of war; London audiences, deeply resenting this ballet from France, rioted and came close to destroying the theatre in their demonstrations. It was the first of many setbacks for Noverre. On his return to France he was unable to join the Paris Opéra, now the leading centre of ballet in the world.

Instead he was appointed ballet-master in the French provincial city of Lyons, where he wrote a book of *Letters on Dancing and Ballets* (published in 1760). This volume had a tremendous impact and was translated and published in many different countries. In these letters, Noverre addressed himself to every relevant topic: technique and style and virtuosity; choreography, scenarios; expression, drama and narrative; design and costume; musical accompani-

The ballerina Marie Sallé (below), a great rival of Camargo's, was famed for the sensitivity of her dramatic performances. Her greatest Parisian triumphs were in the comedy-ballets of Molière and Lully.

Sanquirico's elaborate set (above) for Vigano's ballet Psamos, King of Egypt (1817) was one of the most lavish of its time. Exotic themes and locations were constant obsessions in the Romantic imagination.

ment. He was concerned that the well-made ballet should communicate its theme effectively, consistently, and movingly, without unwarranted 'divertissements' (set pieces whose only purpose was to offer pretty or exciting dancing). This was what he called the *ballet d'action,* a form forever associated with Noverre.

Choreographic innovations

Noverre was also a great teacher. Many dancers with whom he worked would pass on his precepts and schooling. Most famous of these were Gaetano Vestris (1729–1808) and his son Auguste (1760–1842). Brilliant, polished and famously arrogant, both became legends in their lifetimes. Many stories are told of Gaetano's vanity: when a lady trod on his foot and apologized, he replied 'Hurt me, madam! Me! You have just put all Paris in mourning for a fortnight.' He was a dancer of the noble genre; Auguste, of the demi-caractère, was just as vain, pronouncing 'In Europe there are only three great men – myself, Voltaire and the King of Prussia.' Both were also teachers: and in the 19th century Auguste's studio would be a major influence and training-ground for many dancers, teachers, and choreographers of the Romantic era. The male dancer would never be more central to ballet than while these two men held sway.

Another pupil of Noverre's was Jean Dauberval (1742–1806), a leading dancer in the demi-caractère genre. In 1789, when he was ballet-master in Bordeaux, he choreographed *La Fille mal Gardée.* This was the first ballet to deal with contemporary, country folk, dispensing with the traditional themes of gods and heroes. Dauberval used the liveliness of his demi-caractère genre and the vigour of the comique dancers, abandoning the noble category completely.

Bordeaux under Dauberval became as much the centre for choreographic innovation as Paris was for dance style. Two men in particular came to study under him: Salvatore Vigano (1769–1821) and Charles-Louis Didelot (1767–1837). Vigano was to be called 'the Shakespeare of the dance' by the French writer Stendhal. The great years of his choreographic career were at the end of his life in Milan, where he combined the grand and dignified classic virtues of Noverre's work with a new intensity of physical expression and a new boldness in his treatment of the corps de ballet (the dance ensemble or chorus).

Didelot took the influence of Noverre and Dauberval to new heights – literally. He was the first choreographer to attach wires to dancers, so that audiences were astounded to find dancers suddenly defying gravity and soaring aloft. He gave ballets a sense of fantasy that looked forward to the Romantic age: he also did much to develop the art of 'partnering'. In the 18th century male and female dancers had co-existed on stage as parallel beings, dancing side by side or alternately. But there was now a new tendency to idealize women in art and, in dance, to have them partnered and often raised aloft by their male colleagues.

Didelot spent most of his career in the city of St Petersburg (now Leningrad) in Russia. During the 18th century Russia had made great efforts to keep abreast of cultural developments in Western Europe. In 1738 a school of ballet and dancing was set up there and it quickly began to match the standards of other countries. Gasparo Angiolini (1731–1803), a contemporary of Noverre and another great exponent of the ballet d'action, worked there for several years. The great tradition of Russian ballet had begun.

Mauro Pucciarelli

Marie Taglioni and her brother in La Sylphide *(above), the first real Romantic ballet. Taglioni played the sylph who lures away a young Scotsman on the eve of his wedding – with tragic consequences. The graceful elegance of her figure, clad in a simple white costume, and the poetry of her dancing, created a new, enduring Romantic ideal.*

Fanny Cerrito, partnered by fellow Neapolitan, Antonio Guerra (left), in Le Lac de Fées *(1840). She dances on point, in shoes specially stiffened with cotton-wool. This technique proved invaluable in the expression of the Romantics' aims, elevating the ballerina above the mortal plane. So much so, that in the 1860s shoes appeared with permanently glue-stiffened toes ('blocked').*

Arthur St Léon performs an athletic 'pas de poisson' (left) in Jules Perrot's La Esmeralda, *a ballet loosely based on Victor Hugo's* Notre Dame de Paris. *The heroine, the famous Carlotta Grisi, looks on. This was a true ballet d'action – choreographed to express the vigour of the plot rather than mere technical virtuosity.*

In France, however, still the centre of the ballet world, the French Revolution of 1789 had brought sweeping changes in its wake and even dance was affected. People from the middle and lower classes now thronged to the great theatres such as the Paris Opéra, which had previously been the haunts of the aristocracy, and dancers ceased to model themselves on the manners of the upper classes and instead demonstrated a more acrobatic style of dance that would excite and thrill their new audiences. The change was violent, and many deplored it. The husband of one of Noverre's ballerinas wrote in 1816:

The dancing is like nothing that I saw between 1770 and 1790 . . . The vulgar public in its red bonnets which has taken over the stalls of the theatre; the dancers from the boulevard, who are presented at the Grand Opéra: they have made people forget that grace used to be the hallmark of the Opéra's performances.

Romanticism and the Prima Ballerina

The turn of the century also coincided with the Romantic movement in the arts, with its new violence of emotion and expression, and its liberation from the precise rules that had dominated art before. In ballet the contemporary themes of Dauberval, the dramatic power of Vigano, the fantasy of Didelot, all pointed the way forward. But it was not a choreographer who opened the door to Romanticism in ballet, it was a dancer.

Marie Taglioni (1804–84) had been trained to bring a fresh new grace of movement to the Romantic style of dance that was becoming popular and would soon dominate the world of ballet. One technical innovation in these years was the use of pointework – dancers rising on the very tips of their toes with the aid of slightly stiffened ballet slippers. Taglioni showed that this need not just be a virtuoso feat but something poetic. With her billowy jump, the flowing line of her body and her softly rounded arms she seemed to transcend the limits of mortal dancing, becoming a free spirit – a magical being. This was emphasized by the delicacy of her costume – a simple white dress or tutu with bare shoulders, tight bodice and bell-shaped skirt flowing from waist to calf-length.

It remained only to find her a suitable role: and this came in 1832, when she danced the title role in *La Sylphide*. The tale of an ethereal winged sylphide who visits a Scots farmer James, inspiring him to abandon home and hearth in order to follow her into her enchanted glade, gave Taglioni the perfect vehicle for her heavenly style. She embodied the ideals which Romantic artists yearned for – she was tragic, alluring, 'otherworldly', unobtainable and free, unfettered by moral or social ties. After Taglioni, other Romantic ballerinas emerged too – in particular, Fanny Elssler (1810–84). Fanny exemplified the more exotic and fiery ideals of Romanticism, with her impassioned acting and sensually appealing dancing.

Dancers such as these gave the choreographer a new impetus to create dramatic ballets. In 1841 Jean Coralli and Jules Perrot choreographed *Giselle* for Carlotta Grisi (1819–99): Giselle, a beautiful peasant girl, falls in love with a young man in disguise, but, on discovering that he is a nobleman, Albrecht, who is already engaged to another woman, she goes mad and dies. Stricken with remorse, Albrecht visits her grave by night; but Giselle has become one of the 'Wilis',

Mauro Pucciarelli

A grotesque costume design for Dr Coppélius (above), the old doll-maker in the ballet Coppélia *(1870). This ballet was choreographed by St Léon, but is perhaps most famous for Léo Delibes's colourfully impressionistic orchestral score. This – the first symphonic ballet music – greatly impressed Tchaikovsky.*

*Degas's **Dancer in her Dressing-room** (above), painted c.1880, takes us behind the scenes of the Parisian ballet. The dancer, standing patiently in her turquoise stiffened tutu, receives last minute adjustments to her costume. The air is filled with an atmosphere of expectancy. Indeed, Degas's dancers will carry ballet into the next century, where a new set of protagonists are waiting in the wings.*

The tiny, leaping figure of the dancer Enrico Cecchetti, caricatured as a grasshopper (right). A brilliant mime artist and technician, he was one of a troupe of Italians who came to dance in Russia.

sensual spirits who by night force men to dance to their deaths. Giselle is torn between her duty as a Wili and her love for Albrecht: he is only too happy to die for her sake and to join her beyond the grave, but she dances with him until the first rays of dawn save him from death's grasp. Jules Perrot (1810–92) went on from this to choreograph other great Romantic ballets in London and St Petersburg, ballets such as *Ondine, Esmeralda* and the great *Pas de Quatre*.

The ballerina had now become the centre of the picture, often appearing as a being from another world; she danced on point. The male dancer was relegated to a supporting role. Ballet had also found fresh sources of inspiration: the supernatural, the picturesque, the exotic, were favourite areas, along with a new interest in emotional and social realism. Ballet music, too, had greatly developed to keep pace with the leaps that were being made in choreography, reaching a climax with the colourfully orchestrated, finely rhythmic scores of Léo Delibes for *Coppélia* (1870) and *Sylvia* (1876).

In Italy, Carlo Blasis (1797–1878) brought the academic teaching of ballet to a new height. He had studied with Auguste Vestris in Paris, and he tried to impose a classical polish and harmony on the more extravagant movements of the Romantic ballet. The books he wrote on ballet technique became leading textbooks in many countries, while the Italian dancers he and his pupils taught became the most strong and dazzling of the era.

The Russian ballet

But it was Russia which took ballet to a new peak of perfection. The man who did most to shape the Russian company and school was Marius Petipa (1818–1910), a Frenchman whose dancing career had taken him to Russia in 1847. In 1869 he became leading ballet-master, and for over 30 years he would rule Russian ballet.

However, the Russian ballet had no great stars at the time. It was Italy which filled the gap. One dancer, Virginia Zucchi (1849–1930), electrified St Petersburg audiences in 1885–6 with the beauty and poetic feeling of her every performance. After her, other leading dancers from Italy followed – among them the tiny, charismatic Enrico Cecchetti (1850–1928), the first Carabosse and Bluebird in *The Sleeping Beauty*, and later a famous teacher in both Russia and Western Europe. Their stature and prowess as dancers inspired Petipa and his assistant Ivanov; the latter created the choreography for *The Nutcracker* and the lakeside scenes of *Swan Lake*. Soon, Russian dancers rose to challenge them, such as Mathilde Kschessinskaya (1872–1971), the first Russian ballerina to dance the Princess Aurora, a performance seen and admired by Tchaikovsky not long before his death in 1893.

But the Russian ballet company that supported the visiting Italian stars was by itself already a great company. Dancing at the Maryinsky Theatre in St Petersburg, it was large, structured in ranks from corps de ballet up to ballerinas, with character and national dancers as well as classical stylists. The great ballets of the 1890s remind us how fully Petipa always challenged his company, providing work for all the performers, testing their range and their expertise.

The great Maryinsky ballets by Petipa and Ivanov, show how far ballet had come by the end of the 19th century. Today they remain masterpieces of the art combining precision with beauty to evoke an elusive world of fantasy.

IN THE BACKGROUND

The American rich in the 1890s

It is almost impossible to imagine the vast personal wealth enjoyed in the 19th century by American millionaires such as the Vanderbilts, the Astors and the Rockefellers. Though some, like Andrew Carnegie whom Tchaikovsky met and liked on his 1891 visit to America, lived frugal lives, others spent on a lavish scale, building themselves immense palaces and entertaining in royal style. They behaved like a new aristocracy, seeing themselves as an exclusive caste – the 400 – above the rest of the American people. With the introduction of income tax in 1913 and the social upheavals following World War One, their pretensions seemed increasingly irrelevant and at odds with American society, and their influence declined. But not before some of them had achieved their ultimate ambition and had married their daughters into the genuinely aristocratic families of Europe.

'High society'

While Tchaikovsky marvelled at the sights and sounds of the New World, a new American élite, the fabulously rich 'Four Hundred', imitated the aristocracy of Europe.

Consuelo Vanderbilt, portrayed here with her son Lord Ivor Spencer-Churchill (left), became the Duchess of Marlborough for a dowry that ran into millions. But this marriage of convenience, which had been engineered by Consuelo's title-hungry mother, came to a sour end in the divorce courts.

'A man with a million dollars', reflected old John Jacob Astor, 'is as well off as if he were rich.' There was no trace of irony in his remark, which provides a fascinating insight into the attitudes and habits of other self-made American millionaires in the late 19th century. They referred openly and unself-consciously to money, their own and others', in a way that would have made wealthy Europeans blanch: 'We are not rich', protested Mrs Stuyvesant Fish on more than one occasion, 'we have only a few million.' To those who could measure their own wealth in tens of millions and even hundreds of millions, a mere millionaire hardly counted as rich.

During the second half of the 19th century, American capitalism spawned some of the greatest personal fortunes the world has ever seen – and such names as Astor, Carnegie, Vanderbilt and, of course, Rockefeller still have the ring of cash, huge quantities of it. The scale of this wealth was awesome. Andrew Carnegie, the greatest of the steel barons, enjoyed during the late 1890s an income averaging $10 million per annum – personal *income* quite apart from anything derived from other sources of his wealth, and this in the days before the introduction of income tax. Carnegie himself was not given to ostentatious living and the equally rich John D. Rockefeller was actually frugal. But they were exceptions. Having set new standards in accruing money, American men of wealth, staunchly supported by their wives, were determined to set new standards in spending it.

Big spenders

These princes of industry began by building themselves palatial houses, since there were no existing palaces for them to inherit or buy. In order to live like a prince when one was not naturally a prince, it was necessary to choose models on which to base princely living. And these models were necessarily offered by Europe, where there was a wide choice available from different societies spread over several centuries. As the great mansions sprang up along the west side of New York's fashionable Fifth Avenue, seven of them belonging to members of the Vanderbilt family alone, the world could only marvel at forms of domestic architecture that defied sober description.

William K. Vanderbilt and his brother Cornelius Vanderbilt II saw themselves best at home in medieval French châteaux, and suddenly there the châteaux were, standing incongruously in Fifth Avenue, staffed by liveried servants and stuffed with European furnishings and works of art. And these were only town houses. William K. had a retreat called Idle Hour on Long Island, which boasted 110

A stockbroker examines ticker tape in an office crammed with evidence of his wealth (right). Enormous fortunes were amassed in late 19th-century America, and the fabulously rich Astor and Vanderbilt families were the twin pillars of the East Coast social establishment (above is J. J. Astor). Both families indulged in conspicuous spending sprees and when William K. Vanderbilt's Fifth Avenue mansion was completed in 1884, he invited the press to view his private art gallery (above right).

Preservation Society, Newport, Rhode Island

rooms, 45 bathrooms and a garage to accommodate 100 of the new horseless carriages.

The ultimate expression of unbridled wealth harnessed to uncertain taste was, however, that uniquely American institution, the summer 'cottage'. The East Coast can be stifling in the summer, and to escape from New York's teeming Manhattan or other large cities made sense, if one could afford to do so. A number of resort areas came into fashion at this time: Saratoga Springs in upper New York State, Bar Harbour in Maine and, pre-eminently, Newport, Rhode Island. It was at Newport that the extravagance of the American 'Gilded Age' unfolded to best, or worst, advantage.

The Newport season

Newport was an old town dating from the colonial period, which was 'discovered' by the rich during the 1870s, and very quickly became *the* fashionable summer address. The simple colonial dwellings visibly shrank before the onslaught of baronial mansions – all of them quaintly called cottages. Some were given fancy-sounding foreign names like 'Bel Napoli' and 'Château sur Mer'; others sported evocative English seaside names like 'Land Fall' and 'The Breakers'; while grandest of all was William K. Vanderbilt's 'Marble House'.

Built between 1889 and 1892, 'Marble House' is a monument to the power of limitless wealth. A wharf, a special warehouse and a huge derrick were specially built to receive shiploads of furnishings from Europe – splendid marbles, carvings, solid bronze dining chairs even, $9 million worth in all. Mostly Louis XIV, with some Louis XV thrown in along with an incongruous dash of Gothic, 'Marble House' nevertheless was and is an extremely handsome building, right down to the driveway constructed of white marble in a rising arc up to the pillared entrance. It is still an imposing sight.

But Mrs William K. Vanderbilt went further. She brought in Chinese craftsmen to erect an authentic tea house, lacquered red and gold, on the cliffs. It was a splendid vision, but there was no way to make tea in it. Undaunted, Mrs Vanderbilt installed a miniature railway between the pantry of 'Marble House' and the tea house, winding round elaborate plantings. Thereafter, her guests were treated to the spectacle of liveried footmen shunting back and forth across the garden, crammed in miniature cars, silver tea services held above their heads.

'White elephant'

Not to be outdone, Cornelius Vanderbilt commissioned the same architect, Richard Morris Hunt, to rebuild his cottage, 'The Breakers', which had burnt down. Whereas 'Marble House' had owed its inspiration to Versailles, this time Hunt set out to re-create the Italian Renaissance in the shape of an over-sized villa, although he was not greatly bothered where he went to buy the Italian Renaissance. Two of the rooms for 'The Breakers' were designed and built in France, then dismantled and shipped to the re-invigorated Newport wharf. As for New World luxury touches, there were plenty. Both gas and electric lighting were fitted. There was, of course, hot and cold running water, while for their baths guests had a choice of fresh or *salt* water.

Quite aside from the extravagant lifestyle associated with such establishments, the mansions themselves struck perceptive observers as curiously unreal and even grotesque – 'white elephants', the novelist Henry James called them, 'queer and conscious and lumpish'. The French writer Paul Bourget tried to analyse in more detail what he found disturbing about a visit to Newport. 'On the floors of halls which are too high there are too many precious

The fantasies and pretensions of America's upper crust were expressed most spectacularly in their Newport 'cottages'. No expense was spared in the construction of the William K. Vanderbilts' 'Marble House' (top), with its magnificent grand staircase (above left). The furnishings alone, including the only solid bronze dining chairs in the world, cost nine million dollars. In 1892 – when 'Marble House' was finished – the same architect, Richard Morris Hunt, set about rebuilding 'The Breakers' (above), Newport home of the Cornelius Vanderbilts, in an equally palatial style.

Persian and Oriental rugs. There are too many tapestries and too many paintings on the walls of the drawing rooms . . . too much rare furniture and on the lunch or dinner table there are too many flowers, too many plants, too much crystal, too much silver.'

Entertaining in style

Extravagant living in Newport only began with the building and furnishing of the cottages themselves. The entertaining was on a scale to match. Mrs Ogden Mills and Mrs Elbridge Gerry, hostesses of note but by no means the wealthiest, boasted of being able to serve dinner for a hundred at short notice and without summoning outside help – 'outside' their own servants, that is, who were legion. A guest at such an impromptu dinner would not have had to worry about taking pot luck. He would find his name hand printed on a place card at the table, along with an exhaustive French menu. He could expect to consume anything up to a 10-course meal, attended throughout by a footman turned out in knee-breeches and powdered hair.

At one particular dinner an artificial stream was constructed in the middle of the table, stocked with vividly-coloured fish. At another, also in keeping with the seaside spirit, there was a huge pile of sand in the centre of the table and the guests were provided with silver spades and buckets. They then

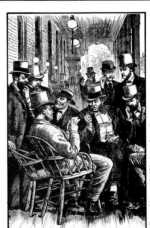

Exquisite horse-drawn carriages, another extravagance of the New York–Newport élite, are paraded in Central Park (above).

William K. Vanderbilt (left) gives race track orders to his betting agents at Saratoga.

The Casino (far left) was one of exclusive Newport's focal points. American high society met and mingled on its velvet lawns.

began to dig joyously through the sand, which was impregnated with emeralds, rubies and other precious stones. Even dumb animals were not spared the excesses of conspicuous generosity. At the celebrated 'Dogs' Dinner', a dining table was removed to the veranda and installed on trestles a foot high. Then a hundred or so dogs attired in fancy dress tucked into a feast that included liver and rice, a meat casserole and minced dog biscuit. More unusual pets also found their exotic masters in Newport. One old dowager was a regular sight driving down the famous Bellevue Avenue in an open carriage accompanied by a pig at her side and a monkey perched on each shoulder.

More usually, Bellevue Avenue and the horse-drawn carriage combined to display Newport in its finest splendour, and America's upper crust at its most aristocratic. Each afternoon following lunch, the sleekest of landaus, victorias and broughams would begin to glide into view. Through the huge

White House Collection

Library of Congress/Aldus Archive

iron gates of 'The Breakers' would come Mrs Cornelius Vanderbilt, while the marble paving stones of nearby 'Marble House' would drum to the hoofs of Mrs William K. Vanderbilt's exquisitely groomed horses. From 'Beechwood' Mrs Astor would proudly emerge, her coachmen and footmen liveried in blue, sharply contrasting with the Vanderbilt maroon. And so it went on, as fashionable Newport came together for the daily promenade along Bellevue Avenue and around Ocean Drive – a 15-mile circuit.

Once into Bellevue Avenue, the pace was brisk but orderly, and the rules clearly understood. Not only was it a social crime to overtake a carriage belonging to someone of superior standing, it was essential to follow etiquette when passing and re-passing one another up and down the Avenue. Mrs Maud Howe Elliott explained the rules to a later generation, who would not have known: 'The first time you met a friend you made a ceremonious bow, the second time you smiled, the third you looked away.'

The 'Four Hundred'

It is curious that the United States, the home of democratic principles, should have thrown up a monied aristocracy so blatantly élitist as this New York–Newport set. The fundamental 'unAmericaness' of such snobbery was personified in the career of Ward McAllister, a man of inconsequential southern background who had managed to pick up a reasonable fortune as a lawyer in San Francisco during the Gold Rush years of the 1850s. For the remainder of his life McAllister was a professional society man – attaching himself to those much richer than himself who readily deferred to his self-appointed role as social arbiter, and even to his outrageous arrogance in proclaiming who was 'in' and who was 'out' of society. In 1888 McAllister coined the lasting phrase 'The Four Hundred', when in an interview with a journalist he solemnly announced that there were 'only about 400 people in fashionable New York

The Bettmann Archive, Inc./BBC Hulton Picture Library

Society. If you go outside that number you strike people who are either not at ease in a ballroom or else make other people not at ease.'

Four years later McAllister took the idea a stage further. He actually presented the *New York Times* with a list of 272 names. These were the people, he claimed, with a fine sense of numerical indifference, who comprised 'The Four Hundred'. It was a strange list, packed out with the fashionable rich, naturally, but woefully lacking the sort of cultural breadth normally associated with social élites, whether based on worldly attainment or even the lottery of favourable

Theodore Roosevelt (above left) became Mayor of New York in 1898 and President of the United States in 1901. Believing that the rich had a duty to behave in moderate and public-spirited ways, he heartily disapproved of the excesses of the 'Four Hundred'. Roosevelt would have had no time for the supremely vulgar Mrs Stuyvesant Fish, dripping with diamonds (above). The cartoon on the left ridicules the pretensions of the Social Register, which included the likes of Mrs Stuyvesant Fish and was an attempt to create an American equivalent of aristocratic catalogues such as Debrett's Peerage.

'The American Girl Abroad – Some Features of the Matrimonial Market' (left). As a result of business-like marriages between American heiresses and European aristocrats hard cash was exchanged for noble titles. Jenny Jerome (below), who married Lord Randolph Churchill and was Winston's mother, was a wealthy American bride.

'Beechwood', to provide the largest ballroom in Newport. It held about 400, the magic number, and for the many years that Mrs Astor reigned supreme in Newport society she was known as 'Queen of the Four Hundred'. Regal she was, from her diamond tiara to her instinctive recognition of her own social pre-eminence. Wealth, of course, was her bulwark against those of humbler station, and wealth was the key to entering her court. But money alone was not enough. Mrs Astor's aristocratic sensibilities could easily be jarred by brushing against those who had made their fortune 'in trade', and in one instance her disdain for freshly-minted millionaires drew forth something approaching humour. Would she entertain the idea of having carpet manufacturers to 'Beechwood'? Certainly not. 'I buy my carpets from them, but is that any reason why I should invite them to walk on them?'

This was just the sort of approach that Fritz Kreisler, the brilliant violinist, encountered when Mrs Cornelius Vanderbilt wanted him to perform at one of her grand evening entertainments. He was quite happy to be engaged for, he said, his usual fee of $13,000. Then Mrs Vanderbilt added her usual rider. As a mere paid performer, the maestro would not, of course, be expected to mingle with the guests afterwards. In that case, replied Kreisler, the fee would be $500.

Money and class were the main passports to high society, but beauty and style could also provide exceptional women with an entrée. After her affair with the Prince of Wales (later Edward VII), Lillie Langtry (far left) had great success in America.

Finding a duke

Mrs Astor was the greatest of Newport's hostesses, but there were several who rivalled her, or at least outlasted her. Mrs William K. Vanderbilt, for example, was not content to live like an Old World aristocrat. She was determined to become one, or at least to become one at one stage removed. In 1895 she married her daughter Consuelo to the Duke of Marlborough. The girl came with a dowry of $2.5 million and $100,000 a year for life – and that she was a bartered bride was not left in doubt by Mrs Vanderbilt. When the circumstances of the marriage were later aired in the divorce courts, she described

birth. The 272 names contained a single author, one editor, a publisher and two architects – a total of five representatives of the intellectual and artistic life of the nation. It is little wonder that the future President Theodore Roosevelt, a real New York blue-blood who could view 'The Four Hundred' from an impregnable social position, dismissed them out of hand for living 'petty and ignoble lives' that had all the sparkle of 'stale champagne'.

McAllister's leading patron was Mrs William Backhouse Astor. The 'Mystic Rose', as McAllister invariably referred to her, extended her cottage, her own role in matter-of-fact terms: 'I forced my daughter to marry the Duke. When I issued an order nobody discussed it. I therefore did not beg, but ordered her to marry the Duke.'

But of all the great society ladies of the time, the most improbable was surely Mrs Stuyvesant Fish. To begin with she had 'only a few million', and the natural disadvantages she had to overcome in order to climb to the upper reaches of 'The Four Hundred' did not end there. She was no beauty, and she made no attempt to offset this drawback by cultivating her mind. Even by Newport standards she was outstandingly philistine — scarcely literate and scathingly dismissive of anything she did not understand, which gave plenty of scope for her acid tongue. It was this latter quality, apparently, a rough-and-ready wit to which she gave free rein, that endeared her to her contemporaries. There is something of the flavour of the woman and her age in a widely-quoted remark she once made to Mr Fish. They had just returned to Newport from New York, and Mrs Fish began coughing violently. 'Can I get you anthing for your throat?', enquired the ever-solicitous Mr Fish. 'Yes you can', she shot back, 'that diamond and pearl necklace I saw today at Tiffany's.'

A graceful decline

During the early years of the 20th century first the influence and then the outrageous wealth of the Newport set began to diminish. For one thing their arch-enemy Theodore Roosevelt now sat in the

A yacht (below left) was essential for anyone who aspired to keep up with the Joneses – or Astors and Vanderbilts as the case was in Newport. Yachting enthusiasts expected to sail among the comforts they were accustomed to on land. Though the rooms aboard were fewer, they were equally sumptuous – Cornelius Vanderbilt's deck boasts oriental rugs (left).

Sundown at Newport (below). The resort's heyday as the playground of the rich ended with the introduction of income tax and the First World War, but it declined gracefully.

White House, and he was more mindful of the obligations that went with wealth and power than of the trappings of privilege. Then in 1913 income tax was introduced, followed shortly by world war and America's emergence as a great power. Among the bustling realities of modern life the pretensions of the self-indulgent rich became increasingly irrelevant, and intolerable.

Sadly for this would-be aristocracy, the wind began blowing the other way before they became so firmly entrenched as to weather the storm. Rich they remained, for the most part, but it was only the daughters they married off to Europe's great families who gained the noble status so many craved: Jenny Jerome, who married Lord Randolph Churchill and mothered Winston, Mary Leiter who married Lord Curzon, May Goelet who became Duchess of Roxburghe and about 50 others who crossed the Atlantic.

As for Newport, it declined gracefully enough thanks to its wonderful climate and the excellent off-shore sailing conditions which guaranteed it the attentions of generations of wealthy yachting men. Indeed in yachting circles, and on occasion beyond to a wider public, Newport became synonymous with the America's Cup, the prized possession of the New York Yachting Club for 132 years.

Index